Space That Carries
Light Forever

SPACE THAT CARRIES LIGHT FOREVER

Robert Rice

Wildhouse
Poetry

Design by Cambridge Creative Group

Published by Wildhouse Poetry, an imprint of Wildhouse Publishing (www.wildhousepublishing.com). No part of this book may be reproduced in any manner without the written permission from the publisher, except in brief quotations embodied in critical articles or reviews. Contact info@wildhousepublications.com for all requests.

Printed in the USA

ISBN 978-1-961741-13-3

For Presence

Space That Carries Light Forever is the second prize winner of the inaugural **Wildhouse Poetry Chapbook Contest**, con/verge/nces. The contest was launched in 2023 and judged by award-winning poet and essayist Jane Hirshfield. Ms. Hirshfield's writing and life-work exemplify the central conviction guiding Wildhouse Poetry, which publishes poetry that explores our connectedness within the wider fabric of life and our attentiveness to furthering the integrity of creation. We seek writers who engage readers' imagination and encourage them to find transformative ways of seeing and experiencing life in the midst of the challenges and complexities facing us in these times. We look for poems with a clear and recognizable voice, one rooted in reality and carried by the natural music of language.

Contents

Every Bird Knows That

Above me the wind is whispering heat
to dry branches promising
a blistered future. Somewhere
a river is trespassing in
someone's house.

The world has dying on its mind
and the sounds in our ears are
nothing like hope.
An influencer opines
our future will be just graffiti
carved in the earth's crust.

That may be true; I don't know.
We have always been impossible
yet here we are.

I should be thinking of this
but among the conifers
a thrush is singing the only song
it has. The only one.
When it stops
it leaves a silence deep as aquifer
and something else, inaudible
but still here, like a silent G.

And I am thinking instead
how that song eases despair. How,
gone silent, it still spins a thread
to the morning of the world.

Migration

The forest is filled with waiting, with
leaf-light and animals moving into shadow—
whatever is empty draws them in.
The light ecclesial; leaves,
with confidence, drop, as if death is a room
they've entered before.

A flock of redpolls arrives, flown in from
nowhere I know. It knows
the way in is not the way out and its terminus,
like prayer, uncertain. They clamor whether
to go on or turn back, though they understand,
something in them does, there is no choice.

Finding no place to leave I watch the stage,
wanting only to touch the necessary.
The flock has by now forgotten nests—
what is gone and not wanted back—
while the trees have solved who they are
by letting what they were fall away.

As for the universe, we know, we think,
it's only information and we're just
one of its hosts: Each morning
calculates the cosmos.
But I can't shake the feeling
there's something personal in all this.

The flock, after brief rest, achieves doctrinal loft
and flies away from the setting sun as if
it's looking for other sources of light,
an unbroken world. For home.

Yes.

Here Is Your Beginning, Ended

—after Jane Rohrer

Thirty years, something like,
we lived in these mountains,
for the trails disappearing into woods,
stream water tumbling beneath a skim of ice
flowing into distance, distance.
For old snow falling from branches,
chimney smoke drifting away.
And see that log
draped in moss and gravity?

All this vanishing spoke to us of beginning,
somehow. Said we existed, said
we were already on our way
somewhere…. I can't explain it.

Her closet full of dresses still.
Scarf hanging from a hook.

These I can explain.

In Answer to Your Email

The Buddha had no words for what
he knew so when he wanted to say
"Just this!" he could only
hold up a flower. Perhaps what he meant was
it costs us nothing to be born and death
is also free but in between it costs us
everything.

Buson felt that any part of the world
seen completely *is* the world.
Maybe he meant that the keening in
unbearable loss by a woman kneeling
on rubble echoes back in the scream
of a hawk soaring its high circles
of gladness above her.

Most of last night I was thinking
all of this is beyond me.
I will never find the answers
Buson and the Buddha found
but sometimes I think
it might be enough to just
outlive the questions.

Today the sunlight chasing its shadows
through their silence across the cottonwoods
has led me to believe
what I can never know.

Tell them you forgive them.

The Poem Tries for a Plausible Translation

I was thinking today of all the languages
that have gone silent. There must be thousands.
They must have had words for everything

we've forgotten. One language knew the word for
"a day with shadows in its arms." One had the word
for "cloud animals moving over the mountain."

One word opened the Secret.
Another called in every hidden thing
but one. And one was used only to mention
"the road where the nameless walks."

Today I was listening among the babble
in the market. I was listening for a word
I'm trying to remember.

I heard the word for profit. I heard
the word for power. I heard, finally,
the wind as it leaves. And that bird.

It sounded like good-bye.

Feeling as Alone as the One Finger I Showed Him

Eventually you will think about space.
I don't mean the emptiness
we are all made of, although this, too,
must someday be considered,
nor do I mean what's out there (or isn't)
past the envelope of air around our earth.

I mean, I think,
the pure and featureless place
between things—call it
what you like: eternal container or
fanciful construct of mind.
Without it we have no here,
no there, and so no me, no you.

What are the words for this?
I live here now
and what separates me
does not save me from
the crushing weight of the practical world.

Cantus for Still Water

I: River

This business of water flowing
always toward some farther-off place—
I'm beginning to think it's no accident.

If we walked up that road and watched
firs beside it turn to dust,
if we stood stock-still and listened,
the slow breaking-apart of stones
would tell us how it is with our lives
and we would come at last to this stream,
surface streaked and riffled,
one of the ocean's dreaming thoughts.

What I'm hoping is
here we are born as the earth.
What I'm hoping: things indifferent to us
will save us in the end.

Say what you want to,
everything here is scripture:
the way water slides from alder leaves,
the way small waves wash a streambed rock,
the way outstretched arms of that conifer
brush the current,
longing to follow the water downstream.

All I know today: I want to be rain.

II: Bridge

You know how it is:
you walk onto a bridge,
look downstream, then up
and up again, and keep
looking upstream
while the inexhaustible river
flows into you, fills you,
promises everything:
bright birds singing,
angels bringing coffee
with cream, poems
that skim gold
from molten lead.
But you, not convinced,
glance across the bridge
to where the grade descends,
and the river
races away.

III: Lake

Astonishing
how this lake becomes river,
how the first faint stir of current
forms, a push of wonder
out of stillness, emerges
from clear, silent water
to dance its descent,
taming the sharp turns swiftly
in language we all understand.
It takes no time to be lake

but the river
scouring the banks for cargo
makes me believe it's possible,
my life.
I pick out stones, plans,
drop in hours.
What I mean to have I can.
I need only movement and
something I forget.

So why just now
as I walk the edge content,
almost, does longing lift me
toward the unthinking lake?
It knows only itself.
Wanting it is like waiting
for a lover who doesn't come.

Never mind, the river says,
what difference where you live?
I will empty the lake soon.
It races into sunlight, lighting fires
in every room of its body
while the lake goes on solving nothing,
alone in shadow and full.

Schrodinger's Cat

Are stars as lonely as they look?
We are their children. They watch us
with longing, luminous
in the thoughtful night. Sometimes

I lose track of myself and think
of us, all the ways we are broken.
Are we as lonely as we look?
We watch each other with longing.

Let me start again. The earth
is full of voices that call to us
with longing. This is all I will say
of our situation. Anger

over grief, terror in full throat,
we carry on not knowing
if the cat is alive or dead. (Either way
the cat doesn't care what we know.)

This is how we carry on. Phones
in one hand, distractions
in the other we fall into darkness bespoke,
the nil that spins the galaxies.

Are we measured in the dark?
We might live but then again
a star might whisper *zero*
and welcome us home
is what I'm trying to say.

How We Look for Meaning in Such Stillness, in Such Light

A sparrow builds a nest. A stream flows.
Clouds form and fade. Notice
that this can never be enough. Notice how
something always must be added:
our longings, our sorrows,
the magnitude of our beliefs.

Wolves bring down a deer. Ravens gather.
I am not apart from this. Sunlight
falls everywhere on the water.
Am I waiting for instructions?

This morning I saw a fawn slip
from a doe, open its eyes.
The doe licked him
with love, with patience.
There was no story. No promise.

But there was a wind-bent spruce,
the sparrow in it building its nest.
And there is us, living
with my heart inside this world.

Report from the River

Light begins deep in the sun and needs
a million years, give or take, to find its way out
then only eight minutes to touch us and even less
to sweep past us into the black wind of space
that carries it forever.

But that's not the point. I should have begun:
What are we doing here?

It seems we're a compromise; split
before we're born, singleness
surrendered in exchange for being, as if
whatever sparked us into life
was only half convinced it was a good idea,
the other half fighting tooth and nail
for Nothing.

Being having won, barely,
we're dumped onto an unmarked plain,
little to go by. So we're here.
It's too late to change that, but
what else must we surrender?

Was it Heisenberg who said
we can know who we are or what
we're thinking but not both?
That we only remember love when
guilt grows stronger than hate?

I should have also mentioned that
deep in our emptiness where time
doesn't move, the din of our lives
becomes song. For evidence of this
spend time with birds, with trees,
a trout's sudden lift into light.

To My Grandson

Dear Jacob,

Remember having breakfast with our friend,
the creek? I'm here now, scraps and ribbons
at play in the lingering dusk. Below me
the stream bends, presses against
my belief. Together we're trying to outstare
the mountains. We're not winning.

Allowing now for what our days must come to,
all the same I am here. I am here
to slip, to drift between what is
and what is not until wind
brings a hint of smoke, summons
my misgivings:
I am old, pinned to place,
creaking like a church pew—
my skeleton and scythe story.

                              Never mind.
An ousel bobs on a rock, examines me:
Step forward for questioning. The air
shimmers with sound.
You will experience this, Jake,
if you're lucky, but you will feel it
differently.

              You know, right?
my apprehension of the future:
Here be Dragons. You should also know
there has always been a warning;

danger to be named later. And then
it's morning, and another morning,
another year, and still.

Isn't that a reason for hope?
I'm not sure. What I *am* sure of is
we claim to own what can't be owned,
tell the truth always
but not by what we say. None of us
blame ourselves for this but we are all
to blame.

I would give anything for you to have
everything I've had. We can't often
choose our burdens. If I could tell you
something useful it would be this:
Buried in this future nobody wants
there will be some joy. Look for it
in corners of days, in sunlight thrown
long across the kitchen, in holding
and held, in simply
rinsing the empties. Breathe
until the world's staccato eases into
whole notes. And you'll be here.

I love you.

Endings

Water's surrendered the streambed, mostly
to moss and drying rock. Bits of brown
stick to work clothes,
and grass, old now,
if crushed or broken, stays
crushed or broken.
Life thins.

>Three hours ago it was heat we suffered
>up on Noonmark. Smell that now?
>She's lit the woodstove.

I have believed in October
most of my life, warmed in the light
of infinite noon.
Now it's the hard time: air
cold as earth, spare
singing of stones, that faint
stain of sun up on the ridge.
Though cottonwood trees
would sleep, their leaves,
caught in some rhythm old as God,
rustle, disquieted,
cling a little longer to green.

>She's pulled the kitchen door shut
>against the evening chill.
>Shall we go in?

We've lost the last whispered light.
Look. Star out.

Each Song, Insistent, Means You Are Here

*"When meaning holds still long enough to get
its picture taken, it is dead."*
—Jan Zwicky

I have wasted a week in the city and
I'm tired. But I also listened to its
anxious music. Sometimes

it entered like raw night, sometimes
pulled me out into coldness, and once became
the discordant harmonies of an MRI.

What it told me: There is fear in the air
that the world is ending.
But consider:

What is true is transient. Time flows
as always from now into nothing,
forms itself into light, into dark with urgency

that has no time for fear. It performs
the universe, emerges the way a mountain
emerges, the way an idea emerges, the way

wind emerges and breaks hard against these buildings,
struggles through alleys as it can, moving always,
like us, toward its dying. Maybe

we have misunderstood. Stuffed
our plans, our egos, the meanings

of our lives into a sack

and we are still left over. Maybe
we have this moment to notice
quiet below the cadence of our fear,

the untethered light of extinguished stars,
traveling forever, sweep past us,
leave its easy song.

And if it all seems pointless

                                    drive out one morning early
away from the binge-talkers, the roughness of crowds.

Walk in the untilled fields, quiet with autumn,
where new snow gives off the light it gathered

on the way down. Geese lift calling and flow south,
doing good the only way they know.

Now is not the time for contemplating spring. Time
drifts here without intention. Release

what your white-knuckled heart
needs to set down. A dozen trees are your witnesses.

Let your life turn and face you. This matters more
than the sum of your distractions. Forgive yourself.

Don't reward your thoughts: The ones that say
yes this, no that? Those thoughts.

When there's nothing left between gaze and leaf
disquiet fades. Astounded and unburdened

you hardly know what you know.
Praise is the peace that begins.

It's the last day

of February. Snow on the ground
measured in feet. Bullying blue sky, an arctic wind.
There's a blizzard in the forecast yet the sun's pale stare
gives nothing away. In the back yard a brawl breaks out

at the birdfeeder: Finches are harrowing the juncos.
Afternoon sells its light, drags the shadow
of grief across folds of snow. The breath of despair
omnipresent. But

there's something here that feels like spring; or rather
nothing feels like spring—there's an absence,
the weighted indifference of winter lifted;
The fir tree admits it with a bare nod.

I have been careless of my life.
I have worn the clothes everyone understands,
sung songs of useless memories while waiting
for someone to call me and say, "Guess what?"

and my life will change. But today is the color
sadness turns when music is added.
It's as if I have been away a long time,
as if I am laying something down.

It's no use telling me we're doomed.
Soon sparrows will be reading to their young
from the book of seeds and the wind

will touch each separate thing, naming it,
and the thing named will blossom.

I tell you this for friendship's sake:
A moment of great happiness
will shine its light far ahead down the years.
Every day we are shown again how to live.

Iris

Near the fence I noticed its
small, green swords pushed up
through the near-frozen dirt.
It stopped me.

           Sometimes
—not often—
a simple shift of light
will shake and crack
the thin screen of the world. Then each

defended story, end-stopped,
will turn in the faded light of evening,
cross the gray sky in you,

leave no trace.

Tanagers

*"But we were not born to survive
only to live"* W.S. Merwin

Our future has risen like a fist
and it is hard for us now
to admit it is here. Machines digging
darkness, water thawing that was frozen
in another age, air that says
reconsider your choices. There is

a man on TV selling blindfolds, selling coffins
full of money, selling hubris, selling fear.
Selling. All that we do
is touched with shadow yet we stare
transfixed at the lights.

And yes, I take it personally.
This is still my world.

But in the storm's calm eye, light forages
along the aspens and a flock of tanagers
flash yellow and orange, singing
the song they've all agreed on:
It is worth it.

And this clear water—
something kissed by nothing—
flows down from the mountains
to speak in its strange tongue about
what is old beyond knowing, and all day long
in its infinite patience it tries to teach me
the words for *this. Now.*

22

Acknowledgments

My thanks to Jan Zwicky for suffering some of these poems in earlier incarnations.

The title of the lead poem, "Every Bird Knows That," is from a poem entitled "Clarity is Freedom," attributed to Teresa of Avila in Daniel Ladinsky's *Love Poems from God: Twelve Sacred Voices from the East and West* (New York, 2002)

"And If It All Seems Pointless" appeared in *Canary*, 54 (2021)

"Cantus for Still Water" appeared in *Manoa* (Cascadia) 25:1 (2013)

"Each Song, Insistent, Means You Are Here" appeared in *Michigan Quarterly Review* 62 (2023)

"Endings" appeared in *The Broad River Review* 49 (2017)

"Every Bird Knows That" is forthcoming in *Evening Street Review*

"Feeling as Alone as the One Finger I Showed Him" appeared in *SLAB* 13 (2018)

"How We Look for Meaning in Such Stillness; in Such Light" appeared in *Evening Street Review* 16 (2017)

"Iris" appeared in *Silkworm* 14 (2021)

This book is set in Optima typeface, developed by the German type-designer and calligrapher Hermann Zapf. Its inspiration came during Zapf's first trip to Italy in 1950. While in Florence he visited the cemetery of the Basilica di Santa Croce and was immediately taken by the design of the lettering found on the old tombstones there. He quickly sketched an early draft of the design on a 1000 lira banknote, and after returning to Frankfurt devoted himself to its development. It was first released as Optima by the D. Stempel AG foundry in 1958 and shortly thereafter by Mergenthaler in the United States. Inspired by classical Roman inscriptions and distinguished by its flared terminals, this typeface is prized for its curves and straights which vary minutely in thickness, providing a graceful and clear impression to the eye.

Printed in the USA
CPSIA information can be obtained
at www.ICGtesting.com
LVHW041110230324
775320LV00006B/655

9 781961 741133

Return to Homelessness

Vartan Tachdjian MD

NEWMAN SPRINGS PUBLISHING
320 Broad Street
Red Bank, NJ 07701

First originally published by Newman Springs Publishing 2023

ISBN 979-8-89061-170-3 (Paperback)
ISBN 979-8-89061-172-7 (Hardcover)
ISBN 979-8-89061-171-0 (Digital)

Printed in the United States of America

For my parents, Haroutune and Marie Tachdjian

Contents

The First Day

The streets had a sour stench. Urine most definitely mixed with rotting garbage. It was not an unfamiliar smell, and as I made my way to the Sixth Street bridge underpass, it tore at my heart like a forgotten memory. It was not the scent of burning tires from my childhood; it was the smell of poverty that grabbed at me. I stepped carefully over and around the discarded items from anonymous lives—a broken-down rocking chair; a rusted birdcage; a once-colorful quilt now shredded, faded, and soiled; and a child's pink teacup. I passed the shopping carts (a prized possession among the homeless) and a few battered orange traffic cones.

In contrast to my usual shirt, tie, slacks, and signature white coat, I was wearing a thick sweatshirt under a parka jacket. It would be cold in the night, and I'd put on two layers of socks. Without my white lab coat, I would not be recognized as Dr. Vartan Tachdjian or "Dr. T." Earlier, Madeleine dropped me off about a mile away, just past skid row, for me to walk to the Sixth Street Viaduct bridge. Under this bridge in downtown Los Angeles would be where I would sleep for three days.

I put down my backpack, heavy with tent, blankets, and bottled water. Where should I set up camp? Trash was everywhere; homeless camps are an ideal environment for rodents. As always, my thoughts turned to health. Leftover food or human waste—even hypodermic needles—can attract rats, which, in turn, can lead to diseases and infections. I've seen it all—hepatitis, hantavirus, *Salmonella*, *Streptobacillus moniliformis*, *Staphylococcus* infections, and more.

The encampment consisted of about six makeshift homes—weathered tents and various odd-looking shelters made from broken

1

furniture, black plastic cartons, or cardboard, held together under a blue tarp. I noted the seemingly random personal items beside each tent: tennis racquets, bicycle tires, filthy stuffed animals, and a half-dead plant. And then there were tidier spaces swept clean of dirt and debris. In fact, an older woman with her gray hair fixed with two pink curlers was ferociously sweeping before one of the tents. We expect to see homeless fitting a particular personality or pattern of behavior—addicts, mentally ill, and social misfits. However, the majority have been on a path that has led from losing a job to losing their home, losing family connections, and finally losing hope. Loss of an income, a catastrophic injury, or exorbitant medical bills can take someone down quite easily. Maintaining who you once were before becoming unhoused is difficult. The near-constant stress, lack of nutrition and medical care, and violence that accompanies home-lessness can contribute to mental illness, which can, in turn, make it easy to become prey to the drug dealers that roam the streets offering relief in a tiny pill or a syringe.

I settled at the far end of the underpass, not wanting to intrude but not wanting to be too far away from those I would be observing. Skid row traditionally has had all the services necessary, but my concern were the less visible people who chose to be away from the hub—the loners, the ones under the bridges and freeways.

"Hey, Doc!"

I looked up to see a familiar face in the distance. He was standing in front of a stack of clothing laid over concrete and shrubs of weed: Benny and his dog, Scooby. He came limping toward me, a clear plastic bag filled with bottles and cans thrown over his shoulder. Benny was a lanky man of forty, short-cropped Afro and a smile with the whitest teeth. Benny was among the many homeless people I got to know as a doctor working these streets for the last three years. He was born in New York City and had a successful career as an engineer until he suffered a spinal cord injury. Left without a way to fend for himself, Benny ended up on the harsh streets of Los Angeles.

Benny suffered as most homeless have, and yet he had a spectacular enthusiasm that is hard to find among even the best of us. Benny was my guide and my protector. He was the street boss, supervising activities and making sure his peers didn't get out of hand. He was also a hard worker, washing car windshields at the red light, taking bottles and cans to the recycling, or simply helping reset and rearrange a person's tent and belongings. He was always on the go. Benny had created a safe space for us to park our cars and our mobile medical van whenever we'd come downtown. Limping around, he'd set down some abandoned street repair cones. He would even secure makeshift parking spots for my outreach team. He was easygoing— at least on the surface—but I've seen his temper flare when the rules were broken like when someone dumped a pile of garbage in front of him. He wanted to "keep our streets clean." One of his duties, which he took on, was taking trash to the local dumpster. There is a ritualistic agenda that many unsheltered people follow. Adhering to these mundane activities can keep them from falling into a chaotic or meaningless routine. Having a purpose (like all of us) is significant to a person's dignity—and mental health.

Benny grinned as I arranged my belongings against the wall. "You crazy, Doc!"

I returned his smile. Benny was the only one down here who knows of my plan.

At fifty-eight, I had decided to take to the streets or, rather, take on the streets. I was leaving behind all the comforts I had struggled to acquire as a doctor in my life in California. I was leaving behind my wife, Madeleine, who was my rock and supported me completely in this wild endeavor. I was doing this to understand what daily life was like for a person experiencing homelessness in Los Angeles. I had been treating this population for three years, but my eight hours a day were not enough to get the true picture of life on the streets of Los Angeles. I wanted to become one of them.

Yes—maybe I was crazy.

A large man crawled out from a nearby tent, bearlike, and stood up. It's Carlos. His eyes narrowed as he looked at me. There is always a sense of fear of the unknown person amid the homeless population. Someone can be a friend in the day and attack you at night. Stealing shoes and other personal valuable items is common, and fights can easily erupt. An unfamiliar face arouses deep suspicion. Attacks on the homeless are common, and women are especially vulnerable. Living on the street means being hypervigilant at all times. "If they don't attack you, they go stealin' your shoes," Benny has said.

"What the...who the...fuck are you?" Agitated, he pulled out a small metal pipe from his pocket and brandished it like a dagger.

"Easy, cowboy," said Benny.

I recognized the man as one whom I treated for leg ulcers. He had told me he was on meds for bipolar disorder. Now, though, he was clearly *not* on his meds.

The man looked sharply at me, still unsure.

Benny patted me on the back. "He's cool."

The man slipped his pipe back in his pocket. I took a bottle of water from my backpack and handed it to him. He took it, nodded, and retreated back toward his tent, cursing under his breath.

Benny turned to me. "Doc, you sure you know what you're getting yourself into?"

I nodded, but no, truthfully, I had no idea. I did know one thing, though, the night would be very long.

Sleeping on the street

The First Night

I leaned against the cement wall. I had no appetite though Madeleine had insisted on sending me several containers of pea soup. I tried not to focus on the gangrenous wound eating away on the foot of my neighbor. I recognized him as one of the guys I had treated, Larry. He was diabetic, and his vision was failing him. Now side by side, sharing a slab of cement with Larry, I saw him in a different light. He was throwing back cheap whiskey from a bottle.

"It's a cold night, bro, and you're gonna freeze your ass off…I'd offer you some," he said, indicating the bottle, "but times are bad."

I nodded; the cold was biting through my gloves.

He took another swig. What he told me next was astonishing and revealing; he had been drinking rubbing alcohol as his backup when he couldn't get the real thing. I paused to let this sink in—he had been drinking rubbing alcohol! His progressive blindness was from the isopropyl alcohol and methanol, which caused rapid vision deterioration. I made a mental note of this, though it was something I knew I'd be sure to remember when writing up my observations later in my chart notes.

The temperature had dropped, the cement was cold, and I crawled into my tent and adjusted the blanket under myself. There was a sense of community under the bridge—watching people come out of their tents or return from scavenging. Not much dialogue, but a nod or grunt from one to another. Almost like any traditional community—almost. However, looking down at Larry's foot brought me back to reality. I shifted away from the gangrenous wound that was foul-smelling and weeping, in turn heightening my fears of contagion. In those days (1990), HIV/AIDS was still in pandemic mode, there was no solid treatment for it, we were just understanding about the modes of transmission (body fluids), and even Magic Johnson hadn't yet declared his contraction of this infection that spelled out a death sentence at the time.

I suddenly found myself scared of the unknowns that I would encounter in my three days here in this unroofed environment. They say that even newborns like boundaries, which is why they enjoy being wrapped tightly and swaddled. Not having four walls and a roof made me vulnerable. Boundaries give comfort, stability, and protection.

Nighttime. Did I sleep? Not at all. The sounds in the day were almost comforting compared to those of the night. The stillness magnified the human and non-human creatures moving past or around my tent and made me wary and hyperalert. The occasional shouts in the night were terrifying, and the laughter—not joyful but sinister—sent a chill down my spine. The angry words "Fuck you! Assholes… You wanna die" spit out like gunshots that struck an imminent danger response throughout my entire body.

And then there was the unbroken drone of the cars overhead on the bridge and of people returning from a late-night party or starting work at dawn. A parallel universe that, although only a few yards above me, was really a million miles away.

I looked at my watch. It was only 2:00 a.m. The rasping coughs of the people near me led my mind toward bronchitis, emphysema, pneumonia, and tuberculosis—and staying clear of them. Even though I had treated these same people during the day, these new conditions and risks became much more salient when I was one among them. During the day as their doctor, I knew I had the safety of the van (my coworkers and the necessary items of protection like gloves and masks, all in a sterile environment) and an exit plan by the end of the shift.

So here I was, in the middle of the night, finding myself worried about the aerosolized cough particles especially when one of them would smoke cigarettes, marijuana, or crack cocaine. They also became more threatening or combative when they were in an altered mental status. Despite being in close proximity with my unsheltered neighbors and not alone, there was an overarching feeling of loneliness that made every thought and worry amplify in my night brain.

Dawn Finally Comes

I was awake, barely. The cold night air had chilled my bones, so standing up, I was aching all over. Someone had started a small fire, and I moved toward it—my only concern was warming my stiff fingers. The group was talking about where to get meals for the day. Food, housing, and safety are on the minds of people living on the streets. I understood this just from one night. My next priority would be to find a bathroom. Where though? McDonald's might be the best place, but that would mean I'd have to walk about a mile. Nobody here seemed to care about toilet etiquette, as I did. Urinating and defecating were done often in plain sight. At this point, I was not able to relax my traditional bathroom ways. Larry advised me to not leave anything behind, or else it'd be gone when I returned. Theft was always a big concern. Addicts would steal most anything, including old dirty shoes. He had devised something with ropes to secure his belongings near a chain link fence. I packed everything in my backpack and thrust it over my shoulder, carrying the blankets and parka in my arms, and set out for McDonald's. This was not an easy event, and I wondered how I would ever be able to do this for three days without throwing out my back or shoulder. I understood now the prized possessions—the baby strollers and shopping carts. Luck was with me, though, as I spotted a shopping cart along the way. Although one of the wheels was broken, I was able to lift and push it all the way to McDonald's. This was not easy, and despite the temperate weather, I was sweating profusely and red-faced when I entered McDonald's. Once there, I purchased a small coffee and an egg McMuffin and used the bathroom. Never had I appreciated

7

the hot coffee and the relatively clean bathroom as I did that day. Washing my hands and face gave me immense pleasure.

My first day on the street was all about survival. Walking the mile to McDonald's and back while pushing a three-wheeled broken shopping cart over broken concrete and jagged streets was enough for me. I returned to the bridge and in my tent had Madeleine's pea soup. Now cold but still so good!

Benny lived ten blocks from the bridge, and before nightfall, I set out to visit him, again putting everything in the three-wheeled shopping cart. Benny had at one time been an engineer, but a severe back problem and subsequent surgeries left him unable to work. Homelessness soon followed.

Benny had set up his shelter in front of a garment factory downtown. He made some spare cash by washing the factory owner's car once a week and performing other odd and end jobs. After a few months of regularly detailing the car, the owner allowed him to put up a tin-roof shack in the front yard of the factory. Although it was still out in the open, the partial enclosure gave Benny a sense of security, especially at night, which is the most vulnerable time for homeless individuals. In his tin-roof shack, Benny made room for a sleeping bag, some books, and even a small television set he would plug into an exterior outlet.

"Benny, you in there?"

A rustling and then Benny opens the door, which is really a dirty-white blanket thrust over the tin roof.

"Hey, Doc!"

Benny always had a smile on his face whenever I'd see him. My team and I had been treating Benny for hypertension for three years, courtesy of a *sharing the care* program from a pharmaceutical company where I was able to receive free samples of expensive medications. On one particular day, when I checked his blood pressure, the factory's owner yelled over to him: "Benny, ask your doctor if he can check my blood pressure too!"

Benny's response was, "Yes, but to receive care from this homeless doctor, you must be a privileged homeless person like me!"

Benny offered me some tea. Drinking tea with Benny in his small shelter brought back a memory to me—the kettle that was always on when I was a child. Drinking hot sweet tea had always been a source of comfort for me.

From his bookshelf that he made from assorted crates, Benny selected a book.

"I found a book at the Goodwill," Benny told me. "Stephen King. It's pretty good."

Among the stack of Benny's many books, I noticed the works of William Shakespeare and Lord Byron. Noticing that my eyes drifted to the seminal works of literature, he quoted from Shakespeare: "I hate ingratitude more in a man than lying, vainness, babbling, drunkenness, or any taint of vice whose strong corruption inhabits our frail blood."

Benny's knowledge of Shakespeare is something I never expected from someone who had been living on the streets for five years. But it didn't surprise me that he would choose this particular quote since he had always stressed that everyone should have gratitude.

"Healers like you need to continue healing people like me and make healers out of me and my friends, so that we can perpetuate this positive cycle."

I'll be frank, I had to ask him what *perpetuate* meant. English was my fifth language, and I was learning new words from this avid reader and aficionado of literature. I found out quickly that giving is sometimes most impactful as it relates to nontangible acts or ideas. By healing Benny and his friends, I was empowering the needy to help *pay it forward* with waves of kindness. This helped multiply my otherwise solo attempts.

As we sipped the tea, a comfortable silence fell over us. And then Benny said, "Doc, what's your story? You sit with me like it doesn't bother you." I looked at Benny so sincere in his appraisal of me. We were not so different as he had thought. My life began in a tin-roofed shack, not so different from where I was sitting right now.

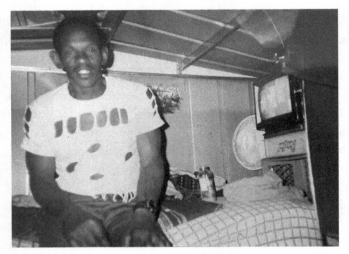

Benny in his shack

The Streets with No Names

You will find as you look back upon your life that the moments when you have truly lived are the moments when you have done things in the spirit of love.

—Harry Drummond, 1851–1897

Beirut's Tiro Camp was filled with Armenian refugees and their children, displaced from various parts of Western Armenia and resettled two borders away in the welcoming lands of Lebanon.

This is where I was born, on July 23, 1933.

In the 1920s, the deep blue waters of the Mediterranean Sea were crowded with tiny boats carrying survivors escaping the Ottoman Empire. My parents were among those lucky enough to make their way through. They had escaped the Armenian genocide in their ancestral land, currently mapped as Turkey, seeking refuge on the shores of Beirut, Lebanon.

Often described as the Paris of the Middle East, Beirut was a bustling city after World War I until a civil war in the 1970s destroyed much of its spirit. As is the case with most refugee stories, the journey that led to my parents calling this city home was not easy.

Cholera and other diseases struck survivors before their boats could reach Beirut's port. Upon docking, my parents, like thousands of others escaping horrific atrocities, were quarantined for forty days.

This was where the medieval Venetian term *quarantena*, or "quarantine," originated. Quarantine meant not only isolation but a taboo and a scarlet letter of sorts. In today's world, if someone tests positive for a highly infectious disease such as COVID-19, he or she is no longer subjected to shame or labeling. Back in the early twentieth century, however, the homeless and refugees were often subjected to quarantine, even if no disease was suspected.

Once the group of immigrants cleared the forty days and showed no signs of disease, they could move to new neighborhoods and begin their lives. Like every other family grappling with this new reality, mine came with literally nothing—no belongings or money.

This made it impossible for my parents, and others without resources or family, to move from the quarantine station. So they stayed. They named it *Karantina*, a play on the word "quarantine." It was clever and at the same time instilled a sense of belonging. This settlement could hardly be called a shelter though; it was built on a landfill created from hazardous waste. But this did not stop the survivors from making this new place *home* in the 1920s.

Karantina was located adjacent to the Port of Beirut, the same site devastated by the widely publicized explosion of August 2020. *Karantina* would eventually become synonymous with the "Armenian ghetto" of Beirut, but it was inescapably the heart of a newly reborn Armenian community. This was nothing new for Lebanon, which was home of the original Phoenicians. As a youngster, I found it fitting to see that my people also rose like a phoenix from the ashes, settling in this jewel city on the eastern shores of the Mediterranean.

In 1931, a terrible fire raged through the *Karantina* settlement, destroying the site and rendering most of the inhabitants homeless once again. Realizing that their encampment had become an eyesore, the residents suspected arson as a means of clearing the refugees.

My parents were displaced again and finally found refuge in a nearby new campsite called Tiro Camp.

I told this all to Benny, and he listened intently to my mini-history lesson, but I could not begin to summarize to him the devastating and poignant moments of the twenty-seven years when I lived in the Tiro Camp.

My home was a makeshift shack that my father had built with reclaimed wood for the walls and corrugated tin for the roof. It was in this three-hundred-square-foot open-space room where my parents, Haroutune and Marie; grandmother, Mayreni; Uncle Onnig;

sister, Ani; and I lived. My parents, sister, and I occupied the upper level, while my grandmother and uncle slept on the ground floor. The blankets we used as our mattresses were folded up and stacked up against the wall until bedtime. We had no running water or electricity. And in one corner of the floor, my father had dug a fair-sized hole in the ground that he cleverly covered with a chicken wire for us to urinate or defecate through. Used newspaper naturally became toilet paper. But sadly, there was no water to clear the mass or the emanating foul odor.

Our home didn't even have an address. We were the forgotten people, living amid a bleak and crumbling infrastructure. Dirt paths led from one tin-roofed shack to the next. Tents spotted the hills. My sister and I, though, loved roaming the camp and picking up objects or stones that we thought were treasures; passing by the houses where gloomy, non-working men watched us suspiciously as they smoked their pipes; passing shacks and tents; and hearing the cries of babies and the rasping coughs from inside. Bronchial diseases, like asthma, were rampant due to the coal fires in the enclosed structures. We ran up and down the dirt paths, oblivious to the cuts and scratches on our bare feet. We children did not concern ourselves with how susceptible we were to tetanus from deep lacerations and fungus from puddles. Shoes were a luxury, so most days, we were barefoot.

We'd politely say hello to our neighbors: "Hello, Manuel." "Hello, Gregory." "Good day, Mr. Krikorian." "Good afternoon, Mrs. Sarkissian." Often, we'd walk to the seashore, and as sexy as it sounds, we did not live *by the seaside* but on a toxic dumpsite that was near the coast. Some of the metallic pieces (or treasures) we found were pieces of shrapnel or rusted iron from boats.

We always quickly ran past the old fisherman, Vaness. He was a gregarious man who sat on a crate most of the day looking out to sea, smoking and drinking from a bottle of Arak—or whatever alcohol he could get his hands on. He scared both my sister and me. Disruptive at all times of the day, Vaness would drink, sing, and sometimes fire his gun into the air at late hours of the night. It was common for people to shoot in the air during celebrations—in fact, they would find just about any excuse to do this (you didn't need a permit to carry a gun). Injuries from stray bullets were not uncommon. With slurred words, he'd yell to us: "Why aren't you kids home helping your mother and father? Go work! Ashkhadetsek!" And he'd take out his gun, and we'd race as fast as we could away, while he laughed uproariously. Sadly, I later discovered that Vaness had died of complications from alcoholism and tobacco abuse.

Aside from Vaness, there were other neighbors to avoid on our walks. Both men and women would get into heated arguments or fistfights over the slightest misunderstanding. Survival mode seemed to be the way of life for everyone at the camp, and this created a camaraderie of sorts and, at the same time, a deep distrust and competitiveness. Space, food, and water were commodities that none of us had enough of, and so often arguments and physical fights ensued. Unlike many of the men, my father tried to keep below the radar, avoiding conflicts—though often it was impossible. Sometimes, my sister and I would find the skirmishes between neighbors amusing like when Mrs. Minassian chased her husband out of the house, throwing pots and pans at him because he came home drunk again. But mostly it was all just stressful. On one occasion, we witnessed our neighbor Minas (we called him "The Rock" since he was built like one) beating his wife and kids with a stick and shouting angrily while savage teenage boys, from a distance, pelted him with little rocks and laughed, mockingly. These sights were common and terrified me. Apart from the incessant fighting and desperate social conditions that are common in refugee camps, the biggest fear we all had was fire. The primary building material for most dwellings was reclaimed wood, and one small spark could easily engulf the camp into flames, especially as water wasn't easily available. During a lightning storm, I would cower under the covers—praying that the lightning wouldn't hit our home and cause a huge blaze.

When my sister and I would return home filthy from our walks but with our hands full of colorful broken pottery shards or glass and metal pieces, my mother would scold us. Water was scarce and rationed once daily, so two dirty children meant less water for washing, cooking, and drinking. The unsanitary conditions posed a constant threat to our health, often resulting in outbreaks of tuberculosis, hepatitis, cholera, malaria, and trachoma. My father or uncle would have the task of fetching the water ration from a cement reservoir, a large cubical structure about forty feet away from us. On occasion, though, when they weren't home, I'd take on the duty. Carrying the heavy bucket of precious water (with help from a friend or two) and not spilling a drop was a chore I took seriously. On my spindly legs, I'd find the best way to hold the bucket, counting my steps as I made my way carefully home. I was a responsible, dutiful child, as was my sister. I had a preternatural understanding of the devastating lives we led, the keen recognition that my family was barely surviving.

Things got even worse during World War II, which broke out in Europe when I was barely eight years old, as Lebanon became entangled between the great powers of the world. Even though it never declared war, Lebanon was handed to France as a mandate by the League of Nations. As a result, the Lebanese people suffered massive casualties and material losses due to its association with the French.

I remember British warplanes carpet bombing our city and blowing up the Shell oil refinery near the seashore, which claimed countless innocent lives. I remember my little sister screaming: *Menk bidi mernink gragi mech* ("We will die in the fire!"). The fumes and the toxic compounds released during those days left an indelible mark on us, damaging our little developing lungs.

One can therefore understand how our major concerns in those days were to avoid the bombs from the sky while escaping the fires on the ground. One single large bomb or several small explosions could easily set our entire camp on fire and instantly decimate its residents.

For instance, on a particularly calm afternoon, a petroleum tanker struck another truck nearby. The explosion caused a giant mushroom-like ball of fire in the sky. After a jolting shock wave, we heard the delayed sound of the explosion, followed by the sudden heat spreading through the air. The following day, the front page of the newspapers featured this tragedy with a photo of the burned truck and the two charred and ejected drivers that laid stiff on the street.

But for us, an added insult to injury was the difficulty in finding food in our neighborhood. Even flour was a rare ration distributed mainly by the mayors in different cities. Our camp was an afterthought for our mayor. Many of us went hungry. The homeless, by virtue of not having an address, could not vote, make changes, or even be heard by default. We felt caged in and constantly overlooked.

And like most refugees, my elders worked very long hours. They would do anything, other than begging, to survive. There was not the relaxed intimacy that defines a family. We barely had time to sit around and chat casually, as there was a sense of urgency to complete tasks; my mother, a strong and confident woman, would sew or cook—or do both at once; my father would repair shoes and fix damages to the shack and the tin roof. He also made cured meat on the side for extra money. My grandmother would help my mother with chores and also spin wool into threads to sell. She always reminded me of our Armenian roots and encouraged me to *mart yeghir* ("be strong"). As for my uncle, he would come home late from his two jobs as a tailor and a cleaner. Uncle Onnig was a talented tailor (later he was frequently commissioned to custom-design dresses and suits for people around the world), and despite having no possessions or real toys, my sister Ani and I always had nice outfits sewn by uncle Onnig. After a dinner of usually bread, bulgur wheat, and lentils or chickpeas, my sister and I would study, sharing the light from the petroleum lamp my mother had lit or a single candle. But often the candle flames would go out from the wind blowing through the uneven wooden planks that made up our walls.

Learning was valued in our family, despite not having any elders representing our community in government, banking, or even sports or the entertainment industry. After all, it is much easier for children to dream of future aspirations if they have role models after whom to aspire. This is the concept of representation being the lens for one to dream. Although I only had a vague understanding how education might change my life, I knew that it was very important to my parents. Their unfulfilled dreams passed on to us to succeed. I'm sure this is what drove them to keep going despite the painful hardships. My mother always found time to stop what she was doing to answer my questions about homework or gently offer life lessons; she was my first teacher and responsible for teaching us the Armenian language and alphabet.

And we did have access to a school—well, it was less of a proper school building and more like a larger shack than the one we lived in, constructed quickly with discarded pieces of wood and tin. We didn't have desks to write on. We had to make do with benches instead of proper chairs, and we sat tightly next to one another in an overcrowded room. We were shoulder to shoulder and noticed the permeating body odors of our classmates. Lice were easily transmitted from one to another, and I even saw a tapeworm crawling up my friend's leg. But the most uncomfortable factor had to be our wet clothes. For during those times, we were drenched either from the sweltering heat indoors or from the rain seeping through the makeshift roof over our shack. The principal of my elementary school was Mr. Yeghia Dolbakian, known for his strict authoritarian practices, which included spanking children on the playground. In sharp contrast to his archaic methods that included corporal punishment were those of Miss Serpouhi, a kind, nurturing teacher who always had a smile on her face. Her name *Serpouhi* was derived from the feminine word for "saint" in Armenian. We would often be rewarded with praise and even small toys in return for our good conduct and behavior during Sunday school and church.

Even at a young age, though, I knew that this school was not the best, nor was it even as good as the school my cousin went to— but my thirst for learning was not diminished.

Our shack in Tiro Camp

Noubarian Armenian School

St. Gregory the Illuminator Church and steeple

With my sister, Ani, during our childhood days

My sister and I in our kindergarten years, with
my dad, mom, grandmother, and uncle

My French Lessons

One sunny weekend day, when I was ten years old, a boy in our streets was reciting a few words in French, *la règle*, which translates to "the ruler," and *le crayon*, which translates to "the pencil." I was mesmerized by how beautiful that language and those words sounded. I wanted to learn more. I ran to my mother and begged her to change my school. My cousin Stepan, six years my senior, attended St. Gregory, a much better school, located in a beautiful neighborhood. St. Gregory was superior in every way, from its three-storied building to the massive soccer field and the chapel where we would start our mornings. There was also a playhouse, electricity and indoor lighting, running water, flushing toilets, and a quiet study hall. The school was founded in 1923 by French and Armenian Catholic priests to provide an education for orphans from the Armenian genocide. It had individual classrooms with a desk for each student. It was the tallest building on the street and a place of refuge for Armenian children.

My mother was able to enroll me into St. Gregory, and on my first day, she walked an hour to get there with me. Father Elie Chad greeted us and wanted to test my proficiency in French. Although I knew some of the letters of the French alphabet, I did not know how to combine those letters to make words, let alone full sentences. Even though I was embarrassed by my profuse sweating from the brisk walk and climbing up the steep hill, I was more fearful of being rejected by Father Chad. So I patiently waited for his verdict. Father Chad informed my mother that I should repeat the seventh grade because I didn't yet master the curriculum.

I began tugging at my mother's skirt and whispered, "Mama, I want to be placed into the next grade higher."

"What is your son asking you for?" asked Father Chad.

"Father," answered my mother, "he kindly requests to be placed into the next grade up, and I believe he will succeed."

To my surprise, Father Chad agreed and took us to the upper class taught by Ms. Victoria Norigian. He warned us, however, that he would pull me back into a lower grade if I failed to perform. Once in class, my peers were reciting from their books, effortlessly. I stood around clueless, not sure what to do. Miss Victoria asked me to read, and when I failed to do so, she announced in front of everyone, "If you do not come with your homework tomorrow, you will return to the lower grade."

I had hoped she would teach and prepare me for the lesson instead of creating a scene in front of the class. It was shocking and difficult to be humiliated like this. I was used to being praised and nurtured at my previous school. At that moment, I had thirty-five pairs of eyes staring at me, some mockingly and others with pity. I felt guilty, helpless, and ashamed, and then—to my utter embarrassment—tears slowly trickled down my face. I couldn't wait to leave.

Once home, and still upset, I asked my mother to take me to Stepan's house. I was not going to return to that humiliating day again. We walked for thirty minutes and crossed the Nahr bridge to reach his home on Nor Hadjin Street. That night, cousin Stepan methodically taught me my homework, preparing me for the following day's lessons. Even after my cousin and my aunt and uncle had gone to bed, I was still reviewing the lesson. When I walked into the classroom the following day, I was still nervous but more confident. Miss Victoria told me to come next to her. I did so, and she asked me to read my homework aloud. She was grading a paper as I read, but when I finished, she nodded and said, "You may stay in the class." Her lack of ebullience didn't tarnish the fact that I knew I had done a flawless job.

I began to perform well academically, and by the time I completed my high school equivalent exams, I was among the top three students in my class. Thanks to my cousin, this demoralizing incident was replaced with happier memories.

My parents were very proud of what I had done. Nevertheless, they had concerns about the cost of tuition. Most students who did not graduate from St. Gregory left because they failed their exams, had disciplinary problems, or could no longer attend due to financial struggles. I, also, had my own concerns—getting to school on time. I had to walk one hour from home to school since my father could not afford the school bus fare. But those two hours of daily walks empowered me to climb the more challenging hills and mountains that life would later present.

Saint Gregory during construction

St Gregory graduating students

What I Never Knew

My parents always answered any question my sister or I had with honesty, even if it was a simple "I don't know." However, the one taboo subject that neither my parents nor my grandma or uncle would ever speak about was our grandfathers. We didn't even have a picture of them in our home. And whenever I asked my elders about them, they would distract me with "Go outside," "Finish your writing," or "Go to bed now."

What had happened to them? Why weren't they with us in the camp? When I was thirteen, though, they told my sister and I to sit with them so that they would tell us about our grandfathers. I was excited, imagining my grandfathers as heroic soldiers or sea captains traveling to far-off places. I was not prepared for the tragic truth: My parents had witnessed their own fathers' tragic deaths in their native city of Kayseri. My grandma and uncle, too, had been there to see the heartbreaking and cruel fate of their loved ones. (Ninety years on, I'm still searching for their tombs, their DNA, their pictures, or any other hint of their existence.) My parents, then, began to tell us about the genocide and why they had to leave their home country.

The Armenian genocide began first as "gendercide." Armenian males in leadership positions were brutally exterminated in front of their families by Turkish Ottoman forces. The majority of those initially executed on April 24, 1915, were graduates from famous colleges, intellectuals, and community leaders. The massacre, the rushed deportations, and the death marches haunted Armenians who survived the genocide, as they witnessed the gruesome loss of their families. This is the day commemorated across the globe as Armenian Genocide Remembrance day, with Armenians marching with slogans such as "Lest We Forget." This is because to this day, the Turkish government fails to acknowledge this atrocity that eliminated a segment of males. What was most damning was the fact that the victims (men, women, and children) were citizens of the Ottoman Empire, and not soldiers or from enemy territories. That is why Raphael Lemkin, the great legal scholar, felt obliged to research and write on this subject. He was also instrumental in advocating for the rights of Jewish Holocaust victims just years later.

What I was hearing hit me hard. It made me realize why there were so few men in the camp—they had all been killed like my grandfathers. Stoically, my elders told me what had happened, but I knew it was an emotional toll even just to talk to us about it. Later, I saw my grandmother wiping away tears.

Fun and Games

Life was difficult at the camp, but all was not drudgery and despair though. I still had a child's predilection for play. In our home, we had a wooden external staircase to walk up to the second floor. But there was also an exposed metal pole in the middle of the structure supporting the weight of the second floor. The drawback to having this support pole was that we couldn't set a table on either floor, as the pole intruded on the small open space. However, for me, it was great. It had just enough open space around it for me to chute down quickly, like a firefighter, from the upper floor. I'd climb up and down that pole to my grandmother's dismay. It may be for that reason that I always came first in rope climbing later in school. I could also sneak back upstairs without being noticed by others outside. I had a hobby—if you could call it that—playing card games. My parents, however, stressed to me and my sister to never bet on these games, as many in the camp would lose most of their earnings in the blink of an eye. I also loved reading, and although books were scarce, I did have one that I read over and over again, *El Cid* (*The Medieval Lord*). This heroic knight became my role model.

Tiro Camp sat near the city's dumpsters and collection site and was a former pigeon or skeet shooting field. *Tiro* is derived from the French expression *Tir aux Pigeons*, which means pigeon shooting. Pigeon shooting was a popular gambling event in Beirut during those days. It attracted hundreds of spectators who thought this would be their ticket out of the slums. Enthusiasts would come from every corner of the neighborhood and sit on special stairstep risers fixed along the fence's inner walks. This gave Tiro Camp the impression of a buzzing stadium or amphitheater. A dozen huntsmen would then take part in the day's event, with onlookers betting on them like prized fighters in a boxing match, except here, innocent pigeons were the victims of an archaic sport.

And then there was *soccer*! Once in a while, Uncle Onnig would find time to teach me to dribble the soccer ball a little better and to shoot from a longer distance. The boys of the camp played a lot of soccer. It was easy to get teams on either side, and we could escape our bleak reality to imagine becoming a "European football star" one day. Sometimes, there was no soccer ball to play with, and that's when our creativity would kick in—we would bring dirty laundry and piece together the heavy cloth, keeping it together with old wire or cord we'd found. We had a couple of soccer players who went on to have careers in other countries, and rumors would circulate about how they made a living playing this beautiful sport. As a child, I fantasized about being one of those soccer stars. However, when I was older—and more practical—I dreamed of becoming a teacher. This was a job where I could challenge others to go beyond what they think they are capable of doing, a job where I could inspire hope. This was a respected profession. It could get me out of the camp, and I could help my family. I sometimes think that should have been my destiny. Nevertheless, I hope I am a teacher to those reading my story here.

The Second Night

I left Benny's at eight in the evening and with effort and fatigue made my way back under the bridge. I noticed a couple of the people I'd gotten to know in the day were gone and a few new ones had arrived. Everyone ignored me as I set up my tent. Once inside and the flaps firmly tightened, fear engulfed me again: the rustling sounds of rodents, the whispers of my neighbors talking to one another—or to themselves—dogs barking in the distance, and the persistent rumble of cars and trucks above me on the freeway. I tried to get comfortable—I knew I had to get *some* rest that night—and eventually fell into a fitful sleep. I awoke with an abrupt start, loud, angry words shot through me like a knife.

"C'mon, man."

"Fuck off!"

"You got money?"

A man's harsh, sinister laughter

"I'll kill you."

"Ri-i-i-ight!"

A woman screams.

I sat up and put on my glasses, ready to what? Run? Where to? The vulnerability I now felt was making my heart beat faster. I had no weapon, no way to protect myself. It sounded like young voices; were they drunk? High? Homeless people get attacked regularly. Many are battered and abused during their sleep, unaware of the surrounding dangers and volatility of their neighbors, earsplitting sounds, cars, and other machinery that may cause accidental injury and death. In fact, the Centers for Disease Control and Prevention has calculated that the homeless have a twenty-year lower life expectancy than those who are housed. That puts the life span expected right around fifty years, in a developed country no less.

I heard the clinking of metal on metal—a gun, a pipe, or a knife—then another shriek from a woman. Was she laughing or crying? I peeked out from a tear in my tent to see three people—two men and a woman—passing around a pipe. Crack cocaine was starting to become popular in the eighties, and I assumed that's what they were smoking. I went through what I recalled the response was to the drug: *constricted blood vessels; increased heart rate and blood pressure; risk of cardiac arrest; acute respiratory problems, including coughing and shortness of breath; and also aggressive and paranoid behavior.* Nobody appeared to be in danger, and nobody seemed to want to attack me. I withdrew under the blankets again. The coughing and hoarse laughter of the three could be heard distantly as they moved away from the underpass. But my mind couldn't quiet.

Fear

The fears of my nights on the streets of Los Angeles were not unlike the fears of my childhood in Tiro Camp. The only difference was that I no longer had the protective arms of my mother to comfort me. When it got dark in the camp, anxiety set in as did the lack of sense of security. There were no streetlights and no lights inside. People walking by our shack would curse, sometimes fight, and throw random trash that would resonate loudly on the inside, as I tried to sleep. Gunshots were sometimes heard. And then there were the rats that roamed freely and carelessly outside and inside our shack, scratching, along with constant buzz of mosquitoes, which left our arms and legs bloodied. There were so many due to the lack of sanitation and proper sewage. My friends and I would joke that the rats had a better life than we did. (To this day, I have a phobia of rodents.) I would impatiently wait for the light of dawn, as that signaled quiet, serenity, and a somewhat calmness on the streets as the troublemakers would be asleep by then. I could also detect danger better.

The anger and violence that often erupted in the camp often had to do with ideological differences. After World War II, the Lebanese people were divided between two factions: one affiliated with the West and the USA and the other aligned with the Soviet Union's socialist and communist ideologies. So it was the norm for fights to occur between people from the two sides, even if they were from the same family. These ranged from fistfights to all-out gun battles in the streets. One of the scariest events was when one of my camp mates was killed by another. I was nineteen at the time, and gangs had been forming at the camp as young men staunchly defended their alliance to the socialists and communists or toward Western-style democracy.

I was in my home, studying, when I heard the familiar angry male voices. Usually, the voices would eventually die down, and peace would settle. However, the voices escalated, and I could hear rocks being pelted—banging against our tin door. I peered out and could see my friends John, Toros, Jacob, and Joseph—all with knives—and a few younger boys pelting stones. My father told me to stay put, but I couldn't. We had all gone to the same elementary school and high school; yet here they were overlooking logic, brotherhood, and friendship. We were all survivors and children of survivors of the first great mass killing of the twentieth century, but all of a sudden, these lives did not matter to one another.

By morning, Toros was dead. Wails from his mother, aunts, and sisters woke me up. No police got involved. John, Joseph, and Jacob were sent to Czechoslovakia to avoid imprisonment or being killed by someone in the camp. And after that, nobody spoke a word of it, though tensions were heightened.

I was afraid that these killings might expand and eventually take the lives of most of the camp inhabitants. I knew I had to get out of Tiro Camp. I knew I had to get my family out too. Life there was now becoming unlivable.

At Midnight under the Freeway

Shivering from cold (or possibly fear) in my tent and not being able to sleep again, I thought about what I had learned at UCLA's Neuropsychiatric Institute—that the abused can easily become abusers. That's when I recognized that my camp friends and neighbors had suffered abuse by the Armenian genocide or even *abuse by proxy* simply by hearing of unpunished atrocities dealt to their ancestors. The anger and hurt repeated to each generation create a deep sadness within families. I believe they could have healed if there had been some recognition, some reconciliation, and perhaps repatriation. It had happened in Germany after the Holocaust. Why couldn't, or wouldn't, the Turkish government—despite pleas from scholars in Turkey—recognize the genocide?

Dawn: Day Two

The bells from a nearby church woke me. As I laid in the blanketed tent, not wanting to wake up and start the day, I thought back to St. Gregory's Armenian Church in the camp where I attended mass every Sunday. Father Krikor, our priest, commanded the most respect in our community, not the least because he was highly educated. The church bells would remind us of the sacred day. I smiled to myself as I remembered the naughty boy that I was—secretly climbing the shaky wooden stairs on Sunday mornings, to ring the bell before the groundskeeper could get to it. Officially, it was his job, but I delighted in "helping out" in this noble chore. The *bell* was actually a massive steel beam that measured two feet long and five inches wide, hanging between two poles, attached by wires at the top.

Faith

My ancestors were deeply tied to the Christian religion. Aside from being actual church builders, they were involved in many faith-related activities. My father eventually became a trustee of our church. My mother dedicated her Sundays to attending Holy Mass at St. Gregory, and she would bring back bread to the camp in order to share the Lord's blessings with those who could not attend. She saved enough money over the years to donate a beautiful chandelier to the church, as a symbol of her love and devotion.

In my earlier years, I served at the St. Gregory The Illuminator Church in Tiro Camp and was a member of the church choir. I also participated in the Divine Liturgy. The church still exists today. Once made of wood, it has been renovated and expanded and is now made of cement. Currently known as St. Vartan Armenian Church, it serves as the headquarters of the Archbishop of Lebanon. In other words, it is the religious headquarters of the Armenian diaspora. Attached to the church was the Noubarian Armenian School and a small adjoining yard. Both the school and the church featured a humble construction composed of wood and tin, like the shacks of Tiro Camp. The church did not have a dome or a cross on it during that time.

8:00 a.m.

My stomach rumbled as I packed up my tent and belongings, and yet the idea of making my way to McDonald's for my coffee, egg McMuffin, and toilet visit seemed like a monumental task. I was exhausted, and this was only my second day on the street. I thought about my home, a hot meal, my comfortable bed, and my lovely wife, Madeleine.

I understood that one had to have a routine on the streets to keep a level of sanity. As I broke down my tent, I saw others going through the same ritual: placing things in large garbage bags or shopping carts or stashing items far away from the scavengers. Will, my neighbor to the left of me, told me he stashes his items behind the old Foot Locker and then gathers bottles. (Only twice had his belongings been stolen.) After that, he goes to the Mission for a hot meal and then sits on a bus stop bench for a few hours, watching the activity on the street. And twice a week, he'll walk the three miles to the recycling plant, where he'll receive anywhere from $2 to $20, depending on his load of bottles for the day. In the evening, he goes to the Mission for another meal and returns under the bridge to sleep. That day, his day got more complicated.

"I got to get my insulin though soon. The VA is a good long walk away."

"Yes," I said, noting his ketotic breath and jittery hands.

I made a mental note of this. Homeless veterans have the good fortune of free medical care at the VA hospital. The unfortunate part is that it's miles away from the Mission, where most get their daily meals.

A Lost Leg and a New Determination

In the Tiro Camp, my childhood friend, Hagop Kantarjian, also suffered from diabetes. He was always fatigued and painfully skinny. There were times he would pass out while we were returning from school. Due to his uncontrolled blood sugar, he developed gangrene by age fourteen. His leg had to be amputated. I remember visiting him after his surgery. Lying in bed, he looked small and wan. Tears streamed down his face.

"Vartan, I opened my eyes to see that one of my legs was gone!"

I didn't know how to respond. I avoided looking at his bandaged stump.

He continued between sobs. "I asked the doctors, 'What kind of life have you left me with? Where is your science and your compassion to save my poor leg?'"

When I walked back home after seeing Hagop, I had a strange feeling—not just of despair but also of a recognition that I needed to do something. I did not know what, but the anger and sadness and the tears and screams, this was not the way other people lived. I was sure. We were all survivors at Tiro Camp, but we—I—needed to be much more than that.

My Introduction to Medicine

The camp did not have a doctor. For emergencies, we'd have to travel miles to the hospital—and oftentimes, family members would get there too late to save their loved ones. The closest thing we had to medical professionals were our neighbors: Mardiros Daldumian, who worked as a bonesetter, and his severely hunchbacked spouse and midwife, Khatoun.

One of my earliest and poignant memories is of my friend Garabed—a passionate soccer player—sitting out a game and holding his stomach in pain, with sweat pouring down his face despite the cool air. Five days later, he was dead—typhoid fever. The bacteria responsible for causing typhoid fever is *Salmonella typhi*. In certain cases, the infection can spread and lead to meningitis and sepsis. It can easily overtake the body unless proper antibiotics are quickly infused intravenously. In the end, the victim of this infection burns up with fever, bedridden and slowly wilting away.

Years later, I can still hear the screams of his mother as they removed Garabed's body from her home for burial. Her agonizing cries that went on all throughout the night have been engraved in my mind and soul.

It was at this point that an idea sprang to my mind: the best revenge was to save at least a dozen other people from the same demise. Not truly believing yet I could be a doctor but very interested in *fixing*, I often asked Mardiros Daldumian if I could observe as he set a broken or dislocated bone. The injuries he treated were usually the result of a fight, a motor vehicle injury, or from the fierce competitiveness at a soccer game. His wife Khatoun's midwifing heroics took place in the privacy of the birthing process, and I would only hear about them from women who witnessed her deliveries. Even that fascinated me.

My mother was the only person to have a first aid kit of sorts that she kept stocked with alcohol, hydrogen peroxide, cotton balls, and sulfa powder. In those days, sulfa was the only form of antibiotic available until the advent of penicillin in the 1940s. Everyone in Tiro Camp admitted that my mother healed the community's wounds like any professional nurse or doctor would in the medical world. In retrospect, she also played the most important role in shaping my path toward medicine. As a medical professional, I could serve my community by helping those who needed it. By age fifteen, I knew my goals of being a doctor would mean financial obligations and would require an arduous level of mental and physical exertion. But these factors could not deter me, and I would simply tell the homeless person in me, *Amenen kesh pane asiga tough ella!* ("Let this be the worst of my problems!")

School and Beyond

St. Gregory's prepared me to be a serious academic student. I became fluent in many languages. I learned science and complex math. It furthered my curiosity about the world beyond Lebanon. The school's mission was to provide underprivileged students with an education and a chance to pursue our dreams. However, the school did not prepare us for higher education. Our teachers, though smart, kind, and attentive, did not have a formal education that was needed to ready us for college. Sadly, many were ultimately set up to fail academically when pursuing a college degree. Moreover, our parents couldn't help us with homework either, due to their own lack of education—so we were stuck. This is a common theme worldwide, where access to education and opportunity are often lacking among (indigent) populations.

The older I got and was able to move beyond my routine of home and school, I noticed a clear difference in living standards between other quarters of Beirut and ours. While people in Tiro roiled in poverty and could barely survive, folks in other neighborhoods had better incomes, beautiful homes, luxurious lifestyles, and opportunities. Their smiling, cheerful expressions, full of joy and laughter, were a stark contrast to the frowning and sorrowful faces occupying ours. In our eyes, any visitor could see our caged souls seeking liberation and opportunities before letting hope dissipate toward a path of learned helplessness. Later, much older, as I looked at photos from when I was a child in Tiro Camp, I would call them "pictures without smiles."

Most of my friends didn't dream of what we wanted to be when we grew up but rather where we wanted to live. We dreamt of new opportunities, better living conditions, and moving to a nicer neighborhood in Beirut. I, too, longed for something better and bigger. Almost an adult now, I felt like an insect trapped in the powerful web of a spider, struggling to untangle myself from my destiny in favor of greener pastures. Tiro Camp had nothing for us—except perhaps the odd vocational career that barely provided for one's sustenance.

I was desperate to break out of this vicious cycle.

I graduated from St. Gregory and completed my certificate. Afterward, I obtained my Brevet diploma within two years rather than the normal four years for the French school system. I was ready to embark on the next phase of my life, scared but hopeful that I would fulfill a dream to become a doctor. I believe that the inner voice pushing me to become a doctor may have been the voices of my ancestors, much like an epigenetic signal bouncing across multiple generations. Most people today describe that as intergenerational trauma. I like to call it a coping and healing mechanism in progress.

The Ultimate Teacher: Life

The following year, I started university.

During registration, we found out that the dormitory rooms were all taken. This was a bitter pill to swallow. Nighttime at the camp was a struggle to focus on reading—the noises from outside, the yells, the arguments, the drunken singing, and the periodic gunshots all contributed to my growing frustration about not being allowed a dorm room. But my promise to myself and to my family to get myself out of Tiro Camp fueled my desire to succeed, which I did; the following year, I came in first in general studies and French literature. I never thought I'd learn French, but it was now my strongest language and main mode of communication.

My French teacher, Brother Felix, asked me to stay after our last class.

"Vartan, I want you to have this," he said as he handed me a book. "I know that beyond your skill as an academic, you have a *cherm sird*" (a compassionate heart).

The book by Dr. Paul Nagai dealt with the heartbreaking detonation of the atomic bomb at the end of World War II and highlighted the aftermath of the bomb. The malignancies and chronic diseases stemming from the detonation were probably worse than the initial event and took many more lives. This book filled me with a sense of responsibility—that we all need to bear—on behalf of humanity. The ramifications and aftereffects from a singular devastating event can perpetuate indefinitely.

Brother Felix

A Day of Roaming the Streets of Los Angeles

I found myself walking toward the Los Angeles Mission where my fellow street sleepers were heading. Like Will, I had stashed my belongings behind the old Foot Locker and hoped nobody would steal anything, though I could always call up my wife and all would be fine compared to Will, who would have to sleep on the cement at night with nothing to protect him from the cold and wind.

The destitution was far grimmer and grimier on Fifth Street—more tents, more trash, and more desperation. Despite the coolish weather, several walked around—zombielike—with barely any clothes; some had no shoes. I imagined many mental health and drug dependency problems among those I passed. It felt different to be walking as one of them as opposed to be walking as a person in authority: one who could help and heal. I was just a lost person among the hundreds on the streets of Los Angeles. It humbled me.

Words from My Grandmother Mayreni: Despair and Hope

The French Medical entrance exams were extremely difficult and all-consuming. I spent most of my summer studying by candlelight in our home, and I often poked my head out of the window to have sufficient light to read my assignments. The oppressiveness of our home became even more so: If it wasn't the sweat from the summer heat, it was the winter rain dripping down onto the pages of my books through holes in the ceiling. My books were almost always wet!

As I sat at the table, struggling to read my textbook by the light of the flickering candle, my sister came and sat beside me and gently asked me what I would do if I did not pass.

"But I will," I said.

She persisted. "You're smart, so much smarter than me, so you can always find a good job."

This made me angry, not because she was putting doubt into my head but because I felt I must pass or else what would have been the purpose of all the years of study I had done? The night before the test, I couldn't sleep. I got out of bed and went outside, walking along the dirt paths that I knew so well, passing the shacks with their tin roofs, and hearing the coughs and murmurs—and cries from babies inside. Tiro Camp—it was a place I loved and hated. I had to pass the test. I had to become the doctor I felt I was meant to be.

The morning of the test was hot and humid. I was sweating profusely as I answered each test question. When I got home, my family was around the table, waiting. I smiled uncertainly. "I did my best." Now, it was just a matter of waiting.

A month later, I looked for my name on the notice board at school. An exuberant laugh erupted from me; I had placed in the top ten among the fifty students accepted!

There were forty of us Lebanese students, and the other ten students were Syrian, Jordanian, Palestinian, Jewish, Greek, French, and Iranian. Despite the cultural differences, we were all committed to the same goal, often driven by a difficult past, to find a place in the world of medicine. And we all knew the challenges that lay ahead of us. Therefore, my enthusiasm for passing was tempered by the reality of what came next.

Medical school is a long journey consisting of seven grueling years of academic study, followed by an additional two or three years of postgraduate training. For a young man like me, who was struggling financially, this seemed exhausting both mentally and physically. No one from my camp had finished college, and no one was even thinking about becoming a doctor, which made my task seem even more daunting.

As I grappled with these thoughts, my ambitions were often thrown into doubt and uncertainty. I contemplated the pros and cons of staying in school and decided it best to further my studies. This was a once-in-a-lifetime opportunity for me, and I wasn't just going to throw it away. Even so, there were days I wanted to give up.

My grandmother, Mayreni, was an inspiration to keep me going. She told me, when I was particularly stressed, more details about her life, which was in a word, *srdajmlig*, heartbreaking.

"Vartan, you cannot lose hope. Hope can sustain you even through the most difficult situations when you want to give up."

She certainly knew this better than anyone. After losing a daughter and a son in the death march through the punishing Anatolian desert, my grandmother had the fortitude to carry and save her two-year-old son, Onnig, from perishing. While marching to survival and freedom, my grandmother was on the brink of death, but she fought to keep herself and her toddler alive. It would be a great injustice to my grandmother's sacrifice if I were to abandon my dream of becoming a doctor, now that I made it all the way to university.

The secret of what had happened to the young Uncle Onnig had been kept from my sister and me. Once safely in Lebanon, my grandmother had placed Onnig at the Bird's Nest orphanage until she could find some means for sustenance and take him back. Onnig spent his childhood at the orphanage and only reunited with his mother after ten years. I discovered this information after visiting the orphanage years later on a trip back to Lebanon. This type of silence (even among family members) is often due to the taboo associated with being a victim.

Not even Onnig himself would speak of the marches he endured, the orphanage he resided in, or his difficult start in life. He kept it a secret from us and even to his children later in life. This was his taboo, and I discovered it only upon visiting the Bird's Nest orphanage. The avoidance of genocide references and the silence around it were getting more noticeable for me. I was annoyed by my family's reluctance to talk about it. I was young and didn't understand how debilitating it can be to relive those harrowing memories.

My grandmother Mayreni and uncle Onnig

Beyond Tiro Camp:
Medical School

Now that I was in medical school, my father realized that I would be surrounded by a different group of peers who were wealthier and who may look down upon me. He had saved some money and bought me an English trench coat and a leather-strapped Certina brand name watch so that I would blend in at school and while riding the tram. I was still embarrassed by my financial situation and my *less-than-humble* neighborhood. And I would hop off the tram before my actual stop so people couldn't figure out that I lived in Tiro Camp. The socioeconomic gap between my home and my university life was widening exponentially. I was living two lives: one within the boundaries of Tiro Camp with poor campmates and one just outside of it with rich schoolmates.

The first year of university was preparatory and focused on physics, chemistry, and biology. That same year, in 1956, I wrote a French poem called *Les Embarras de Beyrouth*, or the "Worries of Beirut," loosely based off Nicholas Boileau's *Les Embarras de Paris*, which got published in the university's monthly paper called *L'Universitaire*.

Father Louis Dumas approached me in class one day and asked me, "Do you know your poem by heart? Can you recite it?"

At the Faculty Day dinner, the announcer invited me to the stage to present my poem. The only problem is, he told the crowd I would be singing rather than reciting it. My mouth suddenly went dry—I was a nervous wreck; I had never performed publicly before, and now I was being asked to *sing*!

Hesitantly, I approached the microphone.

"Um, I'm sorry to disappoint you, but I've never performed on stage before, and you wouldn't want me to sing. Instead, I will recite a poem that I dedicate to you all."

I started out tentatively and then increased in power as I became more confident.

When I finished, there was a sustained applause. This minor accomplishment prepared me to become a better public speaker.

Near the end of the first year, Father Jacques Flamet, my exam supervisor, asked me to pick a paper from the "lucky raffle," as is tradition in the university, to decide what I would be tested on. The paper I picked was about red and white blood cells. When I started to explain the topic, my professor interrupted me and asked me to instead recite a few lines from the poem that I had delivered at the Faculty Day dinner. I thought he was joking but realized that he really appreciated my poetry. After I was done reciting the poem, I then launched into what I knew about blood cells. This moment made me feel more like a colleague with my professor.

All in all, my year went amazingly well.

It was now 1960. I was still living in Tiro Camp. There were times when I had to take a part-time job as a teacher's assistant for financial assistance. In my fourth year of medical school, I started to work at the Khoury Saadé Hospital, where I assisted with surgery.

I went back and forth from the camp and was the lone medical student doing so. I thought often of my grandmother walking the desert and carrying her screaming child with her, and I told myself, "If she can do it, so can I."

Luck changed when Mr. Koumrian, a teacher at Hovagimian Manougian School, offered me an opportunity to teach French and mathematics to the students. He wanted me to become an active part of the community and give health-related lectures to community members. I used my first few paychecks and some of the money my father had saved for me and my family. I found an apartment in Akkawi, a nicer neighborhood near downtown Beirut.

We finally moved out of Tiro Camp.

We were now out of homelessness and living in a fifth-floor apartment. I often asked myself, *Did this suddenly make us more civilized? Did we now matter more to society because we had an address?*

As opposed to our shanty structure, we now had added security, running water, electricity, and a functional and clean toilet, all in excellent shape. Life was suddenly more calm and orderly. I was also closer to my medical school, which made this new home an ideal place for studying. There were no fights, no gunshots, and no raindrops creeping through the ceiling. We also had a big balcony overlooking the beautiful Mediterranean Sea. I would often admire the sea with its ships coming in and out of the port like huge swans on a lake. I didn't know what they were carrying. But through their grace and presence, I was now carrying in me faith, hope, and love that were larger than that immense body of water under a pure blue sky through which I imagined God laughing.

This change was also good for my father because we were only two blocks away from the electrical company where he now worked. However, the most important factor in this move was the good fortune it brought my sister. Now that she had a physical address, it added credibility to her (and our family) as suitors could be more likely to ask for her hand in marriage. Sadly, not many guys would have been interested in her and her great qualities if we were still living in a refugee camp. In the end, she married an older schoolmate of mine—a happy union. This move also enabled me to finally invite my classmates and other guests over to our home. The embarrassment and shame of my previous living situation was lifted. And even though we were renting with just enough to pay on a month-to-month basis, I didn't care. We finally had four sturdy walls, a solid rainproof roof, and a proper bathroom—and I loved it.

Nevertheless, I could never forget where I came from: Tiro Camp in Bourj Hammoud, near the trash dump site, where my roots still resided. I knew that my old neighbors and friends were still in totally unhealthy conditions. I say totally because they were suffering physically as well as psychosocially due to the posttraumatic stress disorder (PTSD), which stays with a person often throughout their entire life—and can be intergenerationally transmissible as well.

I was well aware of the numerous physical health risks at the camp—people dying slowly or sometimes quite suddenly. The most vulnerable were the children and those who were chronically sick and incapacitated. My sense of urgency to become a physician grew. Moving to a better environment was wonderful, but I could never dissociate from those at Tiro Camp. I kept in touch with them, and we would pray for each other. Their support made me more confident in attaining my two main goals: being a doctor and helping the poor. I could now see the light at the end of the long tunnel. I was happy and hopeful that I would be able to make a positive difference in the underserved community.

I diligently continued my evening teaching gig, though some nights were more difficult than others. Mr. Koumrian appreciated my work so much that he encouraged me to apply for a scholarship at the Gulbenkian Foundation, based in Portugal. This would help fund my remaining three years of medical school. Calouste Gulbenkian, or "Mr. Five Percent" as he was known, was considered one of the wealthiest people in the world during the 1950s, having made his fortune in the petroleum industry. Serendipitously, his family originated from Kayseri, and upon his death, he left much of his wealth to Armenian and Portuguese philanthropic causes.

I received the grant!

I felt a huge sense of relief. With my finances secure, I was able to socialize a little bit, rather than take yet another job to cover tuition. It was a time of great fun. One of my closest friends was Moise Shems. We spent a lot of time together while in medical school and even double-dated on a few occasions. The Jewish community that Moise belonged to was vibrant in Lebanon in the 1950s and 1960s.

Moise's father was a family doctor, who had established a clinic for the needy in the Jewish Quarter of Beirut. I sat down with Dr. Shems on several occasions and got a feel for the practice of humanitarian medicine. It was comforting to receive guidance from someone whose career would be my future aspiration.

But as tensions between various groups mounted (at one time, it is said that twenty-seven different religious and political parties were at play) by the mid-1960s, the great majority of Jews fled Beirut to the neighboring and newly formed Israel or to further places like the USA.

Moise eventually moved to Boston. Though we grew up worlds apart, in our respective ethnic enclaves in Beirut, he still remains a great friend, whom I call brother.

With my parents and sister during my college years

Receiving my medical school diploma

The university's soccer team. *Bottom row*: Levon Nakouzian,
Eli Baddour, Tony Sayegh, and Joseph Nakouz. *Top row, from
left to right*: Nikola Mourtsanakis, me, George Kamel, Fouad
Metni, Aram Semerjian, Gee Moraldo, and John Nakouzi

St Joseph University Medical School Graduating Class of 1963

The Los Angeles Mission

Los Angeles Mission serves hot meals Monday through Saturday—breakfast at 5:00 a.m., lunch at 12:00 p.m. or 1:00 p.m., and dinner at 6:00 p.m. or 8:00 p.m. The provision was that you must attend the chapel service. Shower tickets are available daily starting at 10:30 a.m.

I stood in line with an assortment of men, women, and children on Fifth Street, waiting for the Mission to open and lunch to be served. It was a mixed group of desperate people: some clearly in ill health and barely able to stand, others in bad mental health—mumbling, shouting, and cursing. Then there were addicts—I could recognize it in their demeanor: emaciated body, bloodshot eyes, and gray skin tone.

Founded in 1936, the Los Angeles Mission is a nonprofit, privately supported, faith-based organization that serves the immediate and long-term needs of those who are destitute and alone. This has been a lifeline for so many homeless individuals.

My arthritis was acting up, and I desperately wanted to sit down; however, to politely ask someone to "hold my place" could cause an eruption and was simply not done. With people who are hungry or ill—anything can cause an angry confrontation. I saw it many times as a child in the camp. I also knew that I was not alone in my physical aches and pains; everyone would have loved to sit down while waiting for food.

The food I was given—a chili and rice dish, bread, and fruit—was basic but surprisingly good. I thanked the volunteer as she handed me the food. I was grateful for her smile, as well as for the food. Simple gestures, I noted, dignify those who live on the streets.

54

I sat on the curb as I ate. I didn't want to intrude into people's lives, but I did get a sense that many of those who were sitting beside me had come from good homes or once had had a solid profession. One man spoke of his time as a lawyer in Texas. I didn't ask him how he came to living on the streets, but I could imagine various complicated scenarios.

Tonight would be my final night on the street. It had been more difficult than I had anticipated; I had to fight the constant urge to treat those around me who were suffering from various ailments. Tomorrow I would go back to being Doc Vartan again.

Meeting the Maestro

Medicine was my calling, but the arts was what sustained me. I saw science and art as critical to both human body and spirit. In 1961, I had the privilege of meeting with the Maestro Aram Khachaturyan, a world-renowned composer and conductor, credited with symphonic masterpieces like "Spartacus" (revolt of the slaves) and "Gayane" (with the popular Sabre Dance). He was on a concert series through Lebanon and the Middle East, and I was curious about his rise to the top and how he'd achieved so much.

I arranged an interview with him on behalf of Armenian medical students. It felt incredible to sit in front of the legend. I asked the maestro about his thought process and what inspired him to compose his classical pieces.

> My inspiration comes from two places, the people I meet and the places I visit, namely my ancestral lands in Armenia.

He went on to add:

> As a medical professional, you have to be mindful of your own health, but you also have to burn the midnight oil until you complete your work. I put my trust in medical professionals like you, who study and work diligently to save others, so I am not afraid to be sick. In the past I had two bleeding ulcers in my stomach, caused by stress, but treated by wonderful doctors like you!

When he said these words, I felt such a strong rush of being proud of what I was doing. So many of my thoughts about becoming a doctor had to do with jumping over hurdles; I had little time to let it sink in the privilege and pride of being a physician.

Maestro Khachaturyan admitted one of his biggest challenges was to retain his long last name while publishing his first master-piece. He had been advised to change or shorten it, being told that it sounded very foreign. He declined to change his name, explaining, "I refused to water down my heritage." He encouraged me to maintain my "cultures, legacies, and names." Being so close to him gave me a glimpse of what a human being—any human being—can accom-plish if they just set their mind to it.

Crouched in front of the Maestro Aram Khachaturyan

From Theory to Practice

A horrific fire broke out in Tiro Camp's east end, in 1961, rendering the miserable inhabitants into an even more despairing condition. This event both affected and inspired me. During my final year in medical school, in lieu of a thesis, we were given the opportunity to do a research project. I chose a topic on the condition of Tiro Camp fire survivors. With the help of my medical school classmate, Jacques Sahakian, we titled the study *Les Taudis au Liban*, which translates to "The Shanties of Lebanon." The project was well received by our public health teacher professor, Lotfallah Melki, and Jacques to this day remains a friend; we have a lifelong bond.

After completing my fifth year of medical school in 1962 with honors, I received the title of the Laureate of the French Faculty of Medicine. I had also placed first in general medicine, and this earned me the St. Luke Medal from the faculty of medicine.

With this distinction I could have my letterhead and prescription pads emblazoned with *Laureate of the French Faculty of Medicine!* It felt like a dream as I looked back on the small child I once was who could not even read simple words in elementary school.

In my sixth year, I was now ready to do an internship. Father Pierre Madet, the medical school faculty president, approached me with an excellent opportunity to intern at the hospital in Gruyère, Switzerland. This thrilled me. I raced home to tell my family the good news.

My exciting news was met with silence. I had a sinking heart. Then my father spoke.

"When do you need to tell Father Madet of your decision?"

"In a week. Well, probably a couple of weeks."

"I see. There's a lot to consider."

"Yes," I said, "but it's a very good opportunity."

At this point, my mother got up from the table and went into the kitchen.

I experienced a feeling of gloom. The desire to move beyond these borders conflicted with my deep feelings of love and gratitude to the ones who helped me become who I now was. My parents and grandmother and uncle had to overcome the most challenging hardships in order to support my sister and me. It tore at my heart.

I gave them a few days to think over the situation, but the days turned into weeks, and they continued to get quieter and outright sad. When I informed Father Madet about my parents and their concerns, he said that he respected their decision but warned that I may never get an opportunity like this in the future.

Years later, I understood my parents' sadness. Since I was their only son, they feared that I would never return home or worse yet that I would come back married to an *odar* (in the Armenian culture, an *odar* is considered a person outside the group, and it borrows from the term "other"). As first-generation survivors of genocide, the fears of assimilation and integration were a reality that in today's context seems to paint a picture of overbearing and xenophobic parenting. But in reality, the survivor mentality has a lot of posttraumatic stress that comes with it.

With great difficulty, and my own private anxiety, I turned down the internship. As much as career aspirations were a priority, I was also committed to honoring my parents' decision. My next step was trying for an internship with Professor Ernest Majdalani at the St. Thérèse Hospital, located in the Beirut suburbs.

Dr. Majdalani was a famous pediatrician, and this was the branch of medicine closest to my heart. To my disappointment, the two available spots for internship were already taken by my classmates who had applied on time. Faced with no openings for an internship, I paced for what felt like weeks—back and forth in our apartment and on the streets, pondering what I should do. I recalled tutoring the children of Mr. Naseem Majdalani, a minister in government. He was Dr. Majdalani's cousin. I quickly prepared my biography and curriculum vitae and paid him a visit. After a brief chat, he wrote a strong letter of recommendation that he had me read over and then proceeded to seal the envelope that could secure my next career move.

I took the envelope back to St. Therese Hospital the very next day and handed it to Dr. Majdalani. After reading it, Dr. Majdalani asked me to a meeting with Mother Angèlique, the head nurse. She immediately insisted the two intern spots were already filled. But Dr. Majdalani made a compelling argument on my behalf, stating the hospital's workload had increased; therefore, the need for a third intern was not unrealistic. After debating with him, she hesitantly accepted my internship, paving the way for me to pursue my dreams while also securing my parents' approval and peace of mind.

As I sat on a park bench later that day, I thought about my years in school; there were people who provided unconditional support for me—my family, friends, and teachers. There were also those who doubted me or tried to steer me away from my goals, rather to steer me away from the inevitable disappointment. These same folks told me I would never become a doctor since no one from my family—or my entire refugee camp for that matter—had even finished school. *Angareli eh*, "It is impossible."

Finally, there were those who directly tried to defeat my ambitions. Shop owners on our street would go so far as to mock me for walking to and from school every day, telling me that it was a waste of my time. "Why spend so much time in school when you could be working and helping your parents?" Some of my relatives thought medicine was nothing really special. My Aunt Hrantuhi was convinced that her son's job as a mechanic was more difficult than mine. They argued I had it easier solving diagnostic dilemmas because my patients could tell me about their problems, while cars could not voice their complaints to the mechanic. In an odd sort of way, these disparaging comments did not deter me but made me more inclined to keep going.

I was now Vartan Tachdjian MD. I bought a used car—an Opel Rekord—since I was often on call in the middle of the night, back and forth from St. Therese Hospital. I had grown up, left Tiro Camp, and was at last practicing what I love: medicine!

During my internship year, we had a lot of patients who were poisoned by a common insecticide, malathion, also known as Demol. Although malathion is handled with more caution these days, back then, this dangerous chemical was unregulated, with no scrutiny placed on those who purchased and used it, nor any regulation of how much of this poison should be used. The toxic effects of malathion were not common knowledge; as a result, people generally did not seek medical emergency care.

Exposure to malathion can affect the autonomic nervous system, causing drastic changes in blood pressure, heart rate, and breathing rates as well as confusion, insomnia, seizures, coma, and death. I treated over a hundred patients poisoned by this compound. Many more of them died before ever reaching the hospital.

One particular malathion poisoning case changed my medical career. One night, an eighteen-year-old girl named Fatima was rushed by ambulance from the Palestinian camp to our emergency room at St. Therese Hospital. She was in respiratory distress. She had very shallow breathing and was mostly unresponsive, making it difficult to get a good history. No one could figure out how to treat her.

She was salivating excessively and literally foaming at the mouth. Another hint that a patient has malathion poisoning is excessive mucus production with salivation, lacrimation (production of tears), urination, and defecation now called SLUD syndrome. That's because this and other chemicals with this property cause increased secretions from the body, such as the frothing and salivation coming out of her mouth. And in the case of organophosphates, even just contact with the skin can set off this potentially lethal reaction. As I was considering this diagnosis, a paramedic returned to the emergency room. He'd learned that Fatima apparently drank several teaspoons of malathion after arguing with her parents about her lover, whom they did not approve of. Malathion can be fatal in just a few doses, and now we were lucky to know the exact cause of her symptoms.

I cleared the mucus and secretions covering her face and then suctioned her mouth and nose. I began to administer oxygen and connected a nasogastric tube from her nose to her stomach and began to flush out the contents of her stomach. In quick succession, I hooked her arm up to an intravenous (IV) infusion bag to rehydrate her body and administer various medications.

I was certain of my diagnosis of anticholinergic syndrome secondary to malathion poisoning and confidently pushed atropine (to treat her symptoms) and Contrathion (a medication that reverses the toxic effects of the insecticide) through her vein. Fatima went into a seizure before becoming comatose. We tried to revive her with the help of many doctors and nurses. She finally came around—momentarily—only to become comatose again.

We decided to call the head surgeon, to perform a tracheostomy on Fatima. This procedure helped access her airway below the secretions, in order to alleviate her symptoms for a few days before she became comatose once more.

Three days later, after a lot of hard work and around-the-clock care, Fatima regained consciousness. A week after regaining consciousness, she left the hospital physically healthy but would need to deal with the emotional and psychological problems following the suicide attempt.

This incident was the first of many acute poisoning patients I treated during my career.

This young patient could have lived or died in my hands, and I finally had the power to help. In many ways, Fatima gave me the confidence I needed to think independently, act decisively, and maintain certainty, all in the face of the great unknown

By 1963, I was officially practicing medicine and further specializing in pediatrics. I had chosen pediatrics as my specialty and am glad I made this choice. The children were the future, and to prepare them for all that was ahead, they needed good health.

Just after graduation from medical school, I was invited to attend the annual Faculty Day. Finally, I was attending as a proud doctor, alumnus, and faculty member—no longer a student. I noticed the beaming facial expressions and glimmer in the eyes of the new graduates. It was like looking at versions of my younger self. It's at those moments of life when we feel like we are hovering over our past selves. These experiences can evoke a range of emotions: sadness, regret, unlimited pride, and joy. As I was speaking to a new graduate, I was politely interrupted by a young man who introduced himself as Dr. Farid Aboujaoude. He was an obstetrician and gynecologist.

"Dr. Tachdjian, I've heard many good things about you."

"Thank you," I said, pleased.

"I don't know if you have heard about the maternity hospital in Jal El Dib that has just opened?"

I had heard about this newly constructed two-story building meant for mothers and infants. He offered to drive me to the hospital so I could take a look at the facilities. I wasn't sure if he was gauging my interest to see if I wanted to work there or if he was simply wanting to show off the beautiful new building. I didn't want to make any assumptions, but I was eager to see the hospital.

As we toured the facility, Dr. Farid said, "What do you think?"

I was impressed by the level of sophisticated devices like incubators, intubation equipment, and the level of cleanliness.

"You would be treating newborns in the inpatient unit and other children at their outpatient clinics."

I stopped, unsure I was hearing correctly. "So you're offering me a position?"

He laughed. "Of course, why else would I bring you here!"

My interest turned to utter enthusiasm as he and I continued the tour of the facility.

He showed me the room that would be my office, adding that I would get the position of Chief of Pediatrics. I accepted the offer without any hesitation. I had asked God for an opportunity, but He responded by granting me an enormous gift.

As soon as I started at Aboujaoude, my Monday mornings were dedicated to treating underserved patients. During my first three years of work, I did not take any time off, and in a very short time, I was able to grow my number of patients.

Charitable work never ends. The need is great. Much like signing up to become a doctor or a Good Samaritan, embarking on a charitable mission becomes a way of life. Around the same time, the president of the Howard Karagheusian Foundation, an internationally funded outreach center for medical and social services, asked me to teach evening classes about health and health-related emergencies. I happily accepted.

Then in 1963, Mrs. Mona Kordahi and Mrs. Giselle Tasso, whose husbands were well-known architects in Beirut and Byblos, approached me with a philanthropic proposal. I knew Mona from treating her kids during my time at St. Therese. Mona and her friend offered to help me open a free pediatric clinic in Byblos. Byblos is one of the world's oldest incorporated cities, and it's also where the Bible draws its name. Moreover, Byblos has one of the largest orphanages for Armenians who fled the genocide, among them my only surviving uncle, Onnig. Situated just twenty miles north of Beirut, it was a safe haven during many wars.

I could not turn down this serendipitous opportunity. I was enthusiastic about founding the *Byblos Babies Center*, which would come to be known as the BBC. Each Thursday morning, I would fill up my car with medication and baby formula and take them to Byblos. Later, one of my former classmates and St. Therese hospital intern, Dr. Antoine Mouhana, took over my position to continue our work with BBC.

There were many individuals I'd met over the years who showed true altruism.

In another part of Byblos, a Danish nurse named Maria Jacobson had established an orphanage for Armenian children, called Birds Nest Orphanage. Maria was originally sent from Denmark to Ottoman Turkey to work as a missionary. But soon she became a key witness of the Armenian Genocide and shifted her focus to meticulously documenting the atrocities committed by the Ottoman Turks.

She saved thousands of orphans from death or forced adoption and conversion, even though it directly risked her life. She quickly learned Armenian in order to communicate with the orphans, who referred to her as their "Mama." Every night before putting these traumatized children to sleep, Maria would read excerpts from the Bible and remind the children to never forget their Armenian identity and to be proud of their heritage. Her life's mission was now clear, and she found her true calling at last.

In the 1970s, I was asked to perform the mandatory annual physical exams on these children, which I accepted pro bono. After the examinations were complete and reports submitted to the orphanage leaders, I briefly played soccer with the kids—and I felt invigorated even though our side gladly lost the game almost every time.

From left to right, St. Therese's faculty members: Me, Ernest Majdalani, Farid Aboujaoude, Marcel Abinader, Antoine Mouhanna, and my father

My colleagues and Father Pierre Madet

Aboujaoude Hospital

Sharp Lessons from Sharp Tools

One quiet evening at the hospital call room, I decided to take a rare nap. I was suddenly roused by the phone ringing; it was the emergency room calling for help. I rushed there and saw Dr. Aboujaoude and nurses hovering around a teenage boy, who was bitten on his ankle by a scorpion. As he tended to the young boy's wound to extract the poison, Dr. Aboujaoude asked the nurses to fetch him a *shafra*, which means both a "scalpel" and a "razor blade." Time was of the essence. The wound needed to be evacuated of venom immediately to minimize inflammation and damage. The young boy was taken aback by the thought of being cut by a sharp razor blade. He responded by kicking and screaming, refusing the doctor's help, and asking his mother to take him back home.

I approached the young boy gently and asked his name. He replied, "I'm Joe Nahas."

Speaking in my broken Arabic, I tried to tell him he had nothing to be afraid of and would be able to get home soon but must first undergo a gentle treatment to purge the scorpion's poison from his ankle. After hearing about the gentler alternative, the boy appeared to relax. He asked his mother to send Dr. Aboujaoude from the room and let me take care of him instead.

But first, he asked me to come closer and pointed to my last name, which was embroidered on my lab coat: "What a complicated spelling of a name! What kind of name is that?" I told him it was an Armenian last name spelled in French.

That's when Dr. Aboujaoude wanted to make things right with the boy and said he would leave the room if they could shake hands and say *Vive La France* ("Long Live France"), but the boy refused. The doctor asked, *Alors, vive le Liban?* ("So then, Long Live Lebanon?"), to which the boy shook his head no.

Non, Vive L'Armenie ("Long Live Armenia"), responded the boy who reached his hand out toward me again to come closer and tend to his wound.

Once we administered the local anesthesia, I told Joe that the tools I use may be sharp but he will be happy walking out of here. As we performed minor surgery on his ankle, my choice of kid-friendly words seemed to reassure Joe. My next task was to reassure Dr. Aboujaoude so that he would not take Joe's rejection personally.

Several years later in the 1970s, I attended a charity banquet at the luxurious Ecole Hoteliere, a fancy gastronomic venue, in appreciation of a couple who was retiring in Paris.

After dinner ended, a plate full of masterfully curated pastries was brought over to me and my wife. As we savored them, we noticed that no one else was offered these delicacies. When I expressed my confusion to the waiter, he simply pointed to a young man dressed in a pastry chef's outfit, staring at us from a few feet away with a big smile. As he approached us with arms wide open, I read his name on the shirt pocket. It was Chef Joe Nahas! Years later, I was the one reading his last name on his white coat and gesturing to him so that he would come closer. After hugging him tightly, I said, "That was very kind of you, and you have become an artist that I'm proud to know."

He responded, "I guess you inspired me to use my own sharp tools to make people happy."

It was at that moment that I recognized the importance of the continuity of serving. By touching a person's life in a profound way, you encourage that person to do the same, and the compassionate cycle (hopefully) continues.

Losing My Inspiration

On June 16, 1966, everything changed. I lost my mother in a tragic motor vehicle accident. An intoxicated bus driver plowed onto a sidewalk, crushing my mother as she was looking at a window store's display. She was rushed to St. Joseph Hospital, where she died the next day from her injuries. When I saw my fifty-five-year-old mother comatose, I was eerily reminded of the helplessness we face as physicians, as nature often takes its independent and volatile course. Equally significant, I now understood the enormous grief one feels when death comes to a loved one. Losing my mother left a huge void. The world around me felt like it was collapsing. For a while, my life felt purposeless. I could not cope with the idea of losing her forever, especially since her absence had come so violently and abruptly.

My unconditional desire to help others subsided because a part of my soul and motivation also died with her. I made my rounds with impeccable responsibility, but a light was turned off in me. I tried to console myself by rationalizing that God picks his favorite flowers first. But that didn't make up for the deep sense of loss.

I found some healing in the poems she had written and from knowing that her passion lives on through the beautiful torch she donated to the church. My mother had been the rock of my life. I recognized that she would always be close to my heart, but without her physical presence, I felt bereft.

Still coping with the chaotic feelings of shock and sadness, my focus in life had now shifted to consoling my grieving father and sister and to honor my mother by healing the same community she had cared for and supported.

A *mayrig* is like a single point of radiating light in the universe—at least that's how my mother was to me. When I look at other mothers, I see my own mother's face, radiating beauty, goodness, peace, and forgiveness. When I hear other mothers' voices, I hear my mother's own sweet voice. I still feel her compassion and spirit. She was the person who nourished me, educated me, and provided her unwavering loving care and guidance. I can still recall her saying, *Vartan, always be careful out there, but also be brave and take chances, and remain optimistic.* She in turn demonstrated fearless resilience during earthquakes and also when the British aircrafts during World War II initiated air attacks over Lebanon, targeting the nearby Shell gasoline stations, causing fires and destruction. I was witness to all of this. My mother would say, "Don't fear. Those bombs are over there, but we will stay safe here." Above all, my mother enjoyed being of service to others.

Years later, in Los Angeles, I reconnected with former camp residents who recalled my mother's kindness and generosity. In my mother, Mary, I always see the grace of Jesus's mother, and when I remember this, it makes me proud and happy. I only wished she could have lived longer so I could have shown her how I, too, have followed her path of service to others. To this day, I continue to follow her wisdom because she was not only my advisor but also a life force.

To try and overcome my despondency, after hospital shifts, I'd drive my used car to the waterfront. Beirut had, and still has, one of the best Mediterranean vistas in the world where it's easy to lose track of time. It was there that the bleak feelings would lift a little and where I'd feel such profound gratitude for having had a mother such as mine.

Finding Love and Renewal

My car was getting clunky and unreliable, needing frequent servicing. Luckily, my mechanic cut me a great deal in exchange for health advice and care for his family.

On one of many visits to the car shop, my mechanic, Garbis, asked if I was single. I shared that my main goal had been to become financially stable but that I finally had time to meet someone special. He jumped out of his seat and insisted that I meet his cousin Madeleine. He thought she would be a suitable match for me. A few days later, figuring that there was nothing to lose, I went with him to visit Madeleine and her parents.

Madeleine lived with her folks in downtown Beirut. Her father designed and produced handmade women's leather shoes and bags and went by the name of Artine Sacs. Her mother was the force behind the business and doubled up as the salesperson.

When we sat down for a coffee, I learned that she had just recently returned from a trip to France with her parents. Her father drew inspiration for his designs in Europe. While sipping my Armenian coffee, Madeleine passed me a cigarette. The problem was that I didn't smoke. I'm not sure if I was nervous, distracted by her beauty, or just clumsy, but I accidentally dropped the cigarette and its ashes on their small wooden table. The mark it made stayed on the table for years to come, as did the memory of an unforgettable day.

Upon returning home, Garbis asked my opinion of Madeleine. I told him that she barely spoke and I could not offer any feedback. So we planned another visit in order for me to get to know her better.

On my second visit to Madeleine's home, the conversation between her parents and me drifted to their memories of France. Madeleine was merely a spectator. I could not read her body language. But I found a few similarities between us, such as our Kayseri Armenian origins that stress the importance of achievement, service, and eloquence. After a few minutes, I managed to get her to speak. Her voice and classy mannerism immediately spoke to my heart.

After the night was over, Garbis once again asked my thoughts on Madeleine. I told him the same thing, that I barely got a chance to know her better. I asked if I could take Madeleine to dinner, to make it easier for us to know each other. Garbis replied that he would have to ask Madeleine's parents.

Five days later, Garbis explained that Madeleine was their only child and they were very cautious about her whereabouts. However, I was always welcome to visit their home if I wanted to get to know her better. After thinking about this for a few days, I asked Garbis to suggest a new idea to Madeleine's parents. Instead of meeting at their house, I thought it would be a good idea to meet the family at a seaside restaurant for dinner. They accepted.

The following Sunday, Madeleine and her parents, my family, and Garbis and his wife were all present. I could tell that Madeleine was beginning to enjoy herself since she was surrounded by her family. She began to open up to me and befriended my sister.

By the end of the dinner, I decided to ask Madeleine's mother if I could drive her daughter home in my car. She asked Madeleine's father, who took a few minutes to think it over before finally agreeing. As we took off, I decided to show Madeleine the scenic route instead of taking the usual way home. I thought she would be surprised by this. And as we started to converse in French, which I knew she loved at school, she began to show more interest in me. We jumped from topic to topic, and our conversations seemed to have no end. When we finally reached her home and stepped out of the car, Madeleine told me that I did not have to address her in the plural tense (*vous*), a sign of respect in our culture. She told me that we could address one another in the less formal and singular tense (*tu*) and continued saying, "At least you (*vous*) should," in the plural tense.

This small gesture demonstrated her humility, grace, and an aura of simplicity.

We went inside, and her parents did not seem very pleased with me as they had been during dinner moments earlier. The "scenic" drive had taken longer than expected, and they were visibly concerned at their only child's delay. We said goodbyes an hour later.

From that day on, I would send Madeleine a bouquet of flowers every day from the flower shop near the hospital. I often visited her after work and would hand her a new poem I had written for her in French. In return, she always greeted me with her beautiful smile, kind words, and a different flavor of cake that she had prepared for me.

My first date with Madeleine

From left to right at our wedding: Haroutune Ohanian,
Dr. Farid Aboujaoude, Dr. Pascal Bayrakdarian,
Haroutune Tachdjian, me, Madeleine Ohanian Tachdjian,
Veronika Ohanian, and Souad Aboujaoude

Two Needles in a Haystack

Three months into our "courting," as it was called in those days, I proposed to Madeleine. When you know, you know!

We had our engagement party on March 1, 1967, at the Bristol Hotel, surrounded by our loving family members, who showered us with well-wishes and little gifts. It was an ordinary gathering until Madeleine's paternal uncle—the eldest sibling—stood up suddenly and exclaimed: "I have a very important story to share! As it turns out, these two families are not total strangers at all." Tearing up, he told us his mother and four younger siblings left Kayseri right after his father had been killed. His little brother, Madeleine's father, was born during the march down to the sea. He said that they marched down the mountains and through the desert to get to the Mediterranean, leading the way for a few other families. Once they reached the water, they spotted a boat anchored with the French flag on its side. They approached the boat but were denied access. My grandmother, Mayreni, overheard the dispute and was shocked by the captain's demand for money to board the ship. She asked all of the Armenian survivors on board to spare some change so that no one would be left behind. He told us that everyone got on board. As they floated across the sea, they recounted stories of Kayseri. They arrived in Beirut a day later but had lost touch, until my engagement with Madeleine brought these two families together again. I was proud of what my grandmother had done, which made the union between my family's and Madeleine's even more special.

Madeleine and I were happily engaged, and my practice was also going very well, which filled the days leading up to our marriage with tranquility. We were married on May 28, 1967, at St. Nshan

Church located in downtown Beirut, followed by a reception at the majestic Phoenicia Hotel. Even though I was living from paycheck to paycheck, this was a once-in-a-lifetime celebration, and I felt we needed to indulge. For our honeymoon, we traveled around Europe, visiting Rome, Venice, Milan, and London and leaving Paris last. This trip was an experience I'd only had in my dreams.

We returned to reality, and I started to consider different possibilities of where I was going to set up my practice. It would have to be a place where my services were needed the most. It was at this point that I made the decision to set up my practice right next to Tiro Camp. I was back where I first started but now with a purpose to help, to heal. The office was small, just two rooms: a waiting room and an examination room. My goal was to help Armenians who weren't well-off financially but needed medical care. In that vein, being part of various associations and organizations across cultural and socioeconomic tiers allowed me to treat as many patients as I could, in the most efficient and inclusionary manner, especially those indigent patients.

On one memorable evening, we attended a dinner dance gala organized by the Armenian Medical Society in Lebanon. The goal that night was to raise enough money to build a new Armenian hospital. Since I enjoyed a strong relationship with Dr. Emil Bitar, a Health Minister of Lebanon known for his philanthropic activities, I was able to invite him as the guest of honor. My lovely Madeleine gave the opening speech that night. It was beautifully crafted, and I can still hear her words today. I was extremely proud of her involvement with our medical society and, in particular, how she resonated with everyone at the event and ever since that wonderful evening.

And Our Family Grows

The decade that followed was filled with immense joy for me. The very first televisions quickly became popular in Lebanon, connecting and modernizing the whole country. But even more important than a television (wink-wink) was the birth of our son, Raffi, born in 1969, followed by another beautiful child, Mariette, born three years later. I was always on call, but my hours were relatively predictable during the day, and so we rented an apartment near the hospital, allowing me to go home during my lunch break. Because I took no vacation, that daily time with my family was priceless.

Sometimes, Raffi accompanied me to the hospital, where the nuns doted on him. Our days were filled with love and affection, expanding our lives with bliss. Both Raffi and Mariette excelled at their studies and were blessed to have a village raising them into exemplary individuals.

We spent our summers with Madeleine's parents in the hills. In those days, leaded gasoline was still used in cars and contributed heavily to the pollution, especially with warmer weather. Raffi would wheeze frequently from the poor air quality, and I had to treat him in the emergency department more than once for asthma.

On one occasion, Raffi came down with a severe fever and a headache. I admitted him for meningitis, obtained blood and urine cultures, and even performed a spinal tap to determine the cause. It was one thing to treat my patients, but it was another to treat my own son. I was scared that I might not be able to pin down a diagnosis. Two days I stood by my son, watching him grow weaker and waiting anxiously for the call from the laboratory with the test results. Finally, there was the phone call, confirming that he had *Salmonella typhi* growing in his blood culture. Raffi had typhoid fever, the same infection that took away Garabed, my childhood friend! It was frightening for Madeleine and myself—and the memories of my friend dying could not be erased from my mind. So I was incredibly relieved to be able to treat Raffi with the appropriate antibiotics so he could recover from this deadly disease. The idea of losing my son would have been too much to bear. And yet I have seen many brave parents over the years go through such agony.

Raffi, me, and Mariette

Mariette, Madeleine, and Raffi

A Visit to the Motherland

Once both children were old enough to sleep through the night, I decided to take Madeleine on a trip to Armenia, our ancestral country. This would be my first trip to the sacred land of my ancestors. I read up as much as I could on my country and the sites beforehand.

When I stepped off the plane and saw Mount Ararat in front of me, I felt an overwhelming mix of emotions—joy and sadness. What had been an abstract and fairy-tale-like description I heard over and over again in childhood from my parents and grandmother was now a real experience. I was happy to be here, and at the same time, it reminded me of my tragic heritage—and of my mother.

I wanted to visit all the touristic and historic sites that the beautiful country had to offer, such as Etchmiadzin, Tsitsernakaberd, Datev, the Temple of Garni, Geghard, Lake Sevan, and Sardarabad. Both Madeleine and I had a magical time during this trip.

While exploring the city and the countryside, I helped some of the poor and indigent people with whom I shared a very close DNA. I treated some who wanted advice on their ailments. Along the way, I experienced exquisite sensory and spiritual feelings. I felt a reciprocal belongingness between my motherland and me. Simply put, Armenia is an open-air museum.

Among the senses I got to imbibe were the landscape and nature, the flowers and perfume of the botanical garden, and the songs that I sang with school children. I also got to taste the juicy and aromatic apricots that originate from this land, with a flavor like no other apricot anywhere else in the world. Incidentally, *Prunus armeniaca* is the scientific name used in taxonomy and anthropology for this fruit. These all helped me get in touch with my ancestral land. During my life, I always tried to harmonize my and others' physical and spiritual sides of life. Sometimes, it worked; other times, it did not.

The Holy St. Gregory Church in Etchmiadzin is more than 1800 years old and was built by Armenians. Many people don't realize that Armenia was the first Christian nation. Because of its location and constant fear of being conquered, it survived, thanks to its faith that was as solid as Mount Ararat at its core, which is where Noah's ark is believed to have rested.

When I was in St. Gregory, I was struck by the fact that this very old church had been built by my remote ancestors in Etchmiadzin, which was similar to St. Gregory Church in Kayseri built by my more recent ancestors who passed on their Tachdjian name to me. Essentially, I got to transcend my intergenerational being by virtue of these historic places and landmarks. So it is no wonder that this is where I discovered the miraculous balance between the spiritual and the material ingredients of life. It is also where I realized that this kind of balance is what helps prevent natural and man-made catastrophes. It is also what drives human beings to empathize, help, and—whenever possible—treat the sick and poor. And in that same suit, this is what is needed to help house the homeless.

One of the highlights from the trip was meeting His Holiness Vazken I, the archbishop of all Armenians, who for thirty-nine years led the church of the first Christian nation. Our archbishop is the equivalent to the Catholic Pope, and the Holy Church of Etchmiadzin is the equivalent of the Vatican. However, unlike the single Catholic Church, the Orthodox churches have a leader for each division: Russian, Bulgarian, Serbian, Romanian, Ethiopian, etc. In 301, Armenia became the first nation to declare Christianity as the national religion. In fact, Armenian priests inaugurated the Ethiopian church a few years later. Serendipitously, it was the Ethiopian church that sent its priests to reignite the Armenian church in Lebanon after the genocide exterminated much of our leaders.

I first had the opportunity to meet His Holiness in 1956, in Lebanon, while I was still a student at the university. His advice to my class was to read *Man, the Unknown* by Dr. Alexis Carel, which I still have on my bookshelf to this day. Dr. Carel was a Nobel Laureate known for inventing the perfusion pump, which paved the path to organ transplantation.

When the two of us met during this trip to Armenia, I told him that it was a pleasure to see Mount Ararat. He replied, "Years ago, Tsar Nicholas II of Russia visited Armenia to witness Mount Ararat. However, his time here was filled with heavy fog, which obstructed his view. He was asked by the locals to give his views on the historic landmark, to which the Tsar responded, 'I did not see Ararat, and Ararat did not see me.'"

I guess I fared better than the Tsar, in that not only did Ararat and I see each other but we also exchanged our magnetic fields.

The archbishop urged us, as Armenian doctors, to establish a worldwide Armenian medical organization. His wish finally came true when the first Armenian Medical World Congress was held in 1974 in Beirut.

Visiting His Holiness Vazken I, in Etchmiadzin, Armenia

My Professional Role Models

My pediatric career was now at full speed. And although I had left Tiro Camp long ago, memories would often still surface, especially as I saw patients who would remind me of friends from that time. After treating a child with viral conjunctivitis, a common infection of the eye, I recalled a major trauma I had at the age of five.

I had contracted trachoma, a bacterial infection of the eye and one of the leading causes of blindness in the world. I was admitted to the American University of Beirut's (AUB) Hospital and was operated on by Dr. Aram Baghdassarian. Although I didn't get to meet the surgeon who saved my eyes, I did get to meet another hero. As I opened my eyes the following day, there he stood in front of me, Dr. Yervant Jidejian, the hospital's chief of surgery who had saved many lives.

Several years later, Dr. Jidejian became one of my role models. He came to our school to encourage students in athletic endeavors. I'd never met a doctor so physically fit and so full of energy. He explained the benefits of playing sports to stay in shape for our mental and physical well-being.

His dedication to health served him professionally. Dr. Jidejian was the chief of surgery at AUB's hospital for more than four decades, from the 1930s until the 1970s. He treated countless people and also trained thousands of doctors, nurses, and other healthcare professionals. He is credited with the invention of the "rectosigmoid-urethral anastomosis," a complicated surgical procedure used for treating cancer in the bladder area. That procedure brought him worldwide acclaim.

Dr. Jidejian also recruited and coordinated talent from around the world to lecture at conferences where doctors gathered to discuss research and exchange groundbreaking ideas. It came as no surprise that by 1974, Dr. Jidejian would be elected as president of the Armenian Medical World Association.

Dr. Jidejian has also been referred to as a "surgeon to the poor." Known for being both generous and compassionate, he leveraged his talents to provide most of his services free of charge. He believed that all members of society deserved acceptable healthcare. He applied his philosophy to people from all walks of life, from teachers to servicemen, regardless of their political beliefs and ethnic backgrounds.

My second role model was an Armenian refugee and surgical pioneer, Dr. Hampar Kelikian, an authority on limb repair and restoration. Born in 1899, Dr. Kelikian witnessed the murder of his three sisters in Hadjin, during the genocide. He escaped to the USA, eventually serving as a lieutenant colonel and chief orthopedic surgeon in the US Army. In World War II, he treated a young second lieutenant by the name of Bob Dole, who had sustained profound injuries to his spinal cord, arm, and right shoulder during heavy German artillery fire.

Dr. Kelikian transplanted muscle tissue and leg bone into Dole's right shoulder and hand, operating on him seven different times free of charge. Bob Dole would later become a US senator, representing the state of Kansas for twenty-seven years. Senator Dole remembers being told by Dr. Kelikian "to focus on what I had left and what I could do with it, instead of complaining about what had been lost." Dole credited Dr. Kelikian with having an "impact on his life second only to family."

Dr. Kelikian was known for not accepting payment from US veterans and the poor. He sought to have a good working relationship with governmental authorities and improve mental health awareness among the public. His work fueled my commitment to medicine and humanitarian work.

Dr. Jidejian performing the opening ceremony
of the Mesrobian school athletic games

Dr. Hampar Kelikian

War and More Tragedy

When the Lebanese Civil War started in 1976, it wreaked chaos and instability. This was the second major war I had to live through. My wife wanted us to flee altogether in order to keep our family safe. We had learned that Canada was accepting refugees from Lebanon, so I decided to secure Canadian visas.

This was a big life shift, and it necessitated all of us to adapt quickly to a new country, new language, and new way of life. I rented a small apartment in Montreal where I found work as an urgent care director. During that time, I also taught human anatomy at the Université de Montreal School of Medicine and taught first aid and CPR to the organizers of the twenty-sixth Olympiad held in Montreal that same year.

Around the same time, the Aboujaoude Hospital administration and most of my patients urged me to return to Lebanon to care for them. The political climate and security in Lebanon had started to improve slightly after our move to Canada. So less than a year later, we decided to return to Beirut, leaving the Montreal snow behind.

Although the conflicts had simmered down for a short period of time, the war was still looming in Lebanon. Then, as the conflicts peaked once more, I suddenly lost my father on March 14, 1977, to a massive heart attack. This hit me hard.

My father's presence had always provided me with protection and unconditional love. I had come to rely on his support and always wanted to return that favor by taking care of him. As the eldest child, it was my role to validate his sacrifices and struggles for our family. But those hopes crumbled after his death.

In the end, I had to accept my father's death; it was an incredibly painful loss. I am forever grateful to him and thankful for his sacrifices. My father lost his own father, a sister, and a brother at an even younger age—to genocide. He had neither a father, a home, nor country while escaping genocide with thousands of other children just like him.

My father is a true hero who continues to inspire me. He selflessly provided for my education. When other children in the camp were expected to work at the age of sixteen, my father encouraged me to continue my education. Even though he was not schooled, he understood the importance of an education and provided financial assistance even when he didn't have enough for himself.

I can never repay him for all that he has done for me, but I honor his memory with hard work. I have fulfilled his wishes many times over.

It is a reminder. Pay it forward, repay debts, and express gratitude before it's too late. It is an amazing feeling to thank those who helped you along the way and see their face as you speak those words.

As I grieved the loss of my father, the Lebanese Civil War continued. I witnessed unprecedented destruction and brutality and death. In the end, the war took many innocent lives and destroyed Lebanon's infrastructure in the process. Lebanese civilians fled to different parts of the world fearing for their lives. I took my family back to the safety of Montreal, Canada.

While adjusting to a new life in Canada, I received several calls and pleas from Lebanon urging me to come back and help. Since I was unlicensed to practice medicine in Canada, I returned to Beirut, this time without my family, and for the next four years (between 1978 and 1982) commuted back and forth from Beirut to Montreal. Working under a volley of bombs and bullets, I travelled from one hospital to another to treat those injured in the war. It was extremely difficult to be separated from my family and to work in wartime conditions. I was not only experiencing the external turmoil but also internal anguish because of my family being displaced. I also knew Madeleine and the children were worried for my safety all the time.

By the grace of God, I was never hurt amid the violent outbreaks and the constant bombings. I was one of the luckier ones.

I didn't return to Lebanon as a heroic gesture. So why did I do it? Why did I leave my wife and children? It was simple: my history was in Lebanon, and I felt called to serve in the way I knew how—as a doctor. It was my duty.

Lebanese Health Ministry's Medal of Honor in recognition of my humanitarian work and community outreach efforts

A Move to the United States

As the war subsided, once again, Madeleine and I weighed the best options for our family. We decided to leave Canada for the United States.

In 1982, we packed our bags and moved to Southern California, where the climate was similar to Lebanon and where Madeleine's parents had settled a year before. The continued shelling in Beirut had taken its toll on them, and they had no choice but to leave.

We were to uproot our family yet again.

Although we were grateful for living in the USA, we now faced a new and immense set of challenges. The obstacles included learning English, gaining legal immigrant status—the now infamous green card—struggling to pay for our children's education, and obtaining my US medical license. It was an exhausting first year for all of us.

I enrolled at the Kaplan Educational Center to learn English and prepare for the American medical licensure. Although I took English as a second language (ESL), I renamed it "EFL" or English as my Fifth Language. I hired an immigration lawyer to help us gain citizenship. After waiting anxiously for seven months, we were disappointed with the lack of progress. It was extremely stressful since this was the most vital step in establishing ourselves in our newfound refuge.

Moving to the USA stirred up feelings of anxiety, self-doubt, and worry. It was at a time when I longed to be back on familiar ground with those people—my mentors—whom I had relied on for many years. It was a time when I missed the sage advice from my father. It was a time when I had to use all the strength and self-discipline to move forward because my career and my family's future hung in the balance.

I would console myself with the following words: "When has life even given the solution to its problems on a silver platter?" I had to trust that the key to success lies in hard work and perseverance. That was what had gotten me through all my years in Tiro Camp and through medical school and beyond. I would do the same now.

Powered with this mantra in mind, I was able to complete my first Educational Commission for Foreign Medical Graduates (ECFMG) exam in 1984. The following year in 1985, I completed the final steps in the federal licensing examination (FLEX) and was accepted to a one-year combined fellowship in child psychiatry and pediatrics at the University of California Los Angeles (UCLA). That fellowship was contingent on obtaining permanent resident status in the USA. I had yet to acquire my green card or permanent residency; both seemed so elusive.

I traveled back to Lebanon twice, working for three months to help war victims and earn a little extra income for our California subsistence. It was difficult to leave again because I knew I wouldn't be returning any time soon. My new life, the next part of my journey, would begin in the USA.

We were still waiting to hear about our immigration status when I received a letter from the Board of Medical Quality Assurance in Sacramento. It was 1986, and almost a year had passed without me having started the required training program with any hospital. The Board informed me that I would have to retake my medical board exam if our status was still the same. I felt deflated. How could I possibly fix this situation with just a few days left until the one-year deadline?

Miraculously (and it really did seem like a miracle), I received a letter from Vancouver, Canada, asking us to come as a family for an interview for US resident status. We quickly traveled to Vancouver and, once there, obtained the much-coveted green cards, on the last day of my medical licensure deadline.

I wasted zero time returning to UCLA. I showed them my green card and told them I was ready to join their fellowship program. UCLA alerted the BMQA offices in Sacramento that I started their fellowship. My journey toward gaining a US medical license would stay on track, and unbelievably, I made it through. I made it through!

Struggling to Get a Paying Job

When I was accepted for training at UCLA's Neuropsychiatric Institute (NPI), I was expected to complete eight months of training in psychiatry and four months of training in general pediatrics. Training in psychiatry was entirely new for me, and my biggest challenge was the communication barrier I had with the psychiatric patients. English was still a foreign language to me.

UCLA's sprawling campus felt fifty times larger than Tiro Camp; oftentimes, I wandered for more than an hour, trying to find my way. I was given many more responsibilities such as patient evaluation and treatment, as well as mandatory participation in clinical psychopathology seminars, which included heavy-reading assignments. Regardless of how much I read in the massive textbooks and how much didactic information I absorbed, there were still certain scenarios that required me to quickly adapt and apply critical-thinking skills.

Just as I was adjusting, the state of California suddenly canceled all "combined programs," such as pediatrics and psychiatry, leaving many foreign graduates like myself with no place to go.

It was difficult to maintain my optimism and cheerfulness with Madeleine and the kids, and there were times I just wanted to return to Lebanon—to the comfort of familiarity. But I knew that was not an option, so I plowed on.

I decided to contact the director of the NPI fellowship program, Dr. James Simmons III. I explained my situation adding that I was a postdoctoral trainee working for free to obtain my license in California. I let him know that I'd like to continue at UCLA, training under his supervision. Dr. Simmons granted me this vital opportunity.

I pitched the idea of shadowing other doctors through a rotation within the pediatric intensive care unit. I was granted this opportunity by the Chairman of Pediatrics, Dr. William Friedman. However, he made this exception with the strict warning that—due to liability and insurance reasons—I would not be examining or treating any patient. My work was unpaid, but I was happy to be training once again.

During a particularly challenging day with the unit overwhelmed with patients (many in extreme physical distress), Dr. Rick Harrison, the chief of the pediatric intensive care unit, approached me. "Come with me," he said urgently. I followed him to intensive care. He brought me over to a newly admitted patient—a five-year-old boy who had been in a serious car crash. The boy had suffered severe head injuries and had deep lacerations on his face and scalp. "Work up the diagnosis, and present it to the medical residents."

As Dr. Harrison started to leave, I grabbed his arm and reminded him that I was not yet granted permission to treat anyone.

"I'll override it," and then he quickly left.

I felt more than ready and able to treat this extremely complicated case. I ran various tests and exams, sutured the wounds, and coordinated with various specialty teams to stabilize the child to keep him alive. Six hours later, the young boy's prognosis had improved. His overall condition and diagnostic results were reassuring.

I was finally able to breathe a big sigh of relief.

I presented the case during evening rounds, where Dr. Harrison was present. When I was done, he reviewed the chart, and under my assessment note, he wrote: "I agree with the great job done here."

His validation filled me with tremendous pride. This was the first time I was appreciated for my work in the USA. I photocopied his note and took it to Dr. Simmons, to help secure my training and position at UCLA, since I still was waiting to obtain my medical license.

I now needed to travel to Sacramento to meet with Rick Wallender, the director of the Board of Medical Quality Assurance

(BMQA), which is part of the state licensing board. I explained how the fellowship program was to be canceled and about my unpaid training at UCLA for the past nine months. My appeal (which I had practiced in my head) to Mr. Wallender went something like this: "I feel you are penalizing me for my obedience to BMQA's medical licensure requirements provided to me from your office, and which included nine months of post-doctoral fellowship at UCLA...all of which was unpaid. Until now, I dedicated my professional life to help mostly the needy, the disenfranchised human beings. Without a medical license, I will become an aimless and useless person, unable to continue my humanistic mission as a medical doctor. And my vocation will stay incomplete. What do I say to myself, to my children, to my patients?" I wasn't sure I had influenced him, so I added, "What would you do if you were in my place?"

After he left the room for fifteen minutes, he returned and informed me that I could continue my pediatric fellowship in Bakersfield, California. He said this was a quality training program and a UCLA-affiliated campus. Even more reassuring was that I would be relocating just two hours away from my family.

I stood in silence, still processing the momentary joy and victory, which he misunderstood and added, "I understand that Bakersfield is not exactly Los Angeles and your compensation there won't meet your expectations." I firmly shook his hand and told him that I accepted the offer.

With UCLA's chief of psychiatry, Dr. James Simmons

With UCLA's leading nurse Kate Silverman and social worker Alisa Shima

My 36-Hour Workdays

The drive from Encino to Bakersfield was too long, so I decided to rent a small studio there for weeknights and occasional weekends. I was tasked with treating sick children, both inpatient and outpatient. Finally, I was getting paid to do what I loved.

Ironically, at UCLA, I was the pediatrician among psychiatrists, and now at Kern Medical Center, I was a psychiatrist among pediatricians. These two years of fellowship training were difficult for me. By now, I was in my fifties. On some days, I was pushed to complete exhaustion, my body spent and my mind taxed. My shift would end, and I'd feel like everything I had in me was left at work. My vision would occasionally blur from a combination of looking at so many charts and severe sleep deprivation. The eighty-hour work week for medical staff in training was only instituted in 2003. Before then, working thirty hours at a time and logging in one hundred hours a week was not unusual. This was definitely not a healthy lifestyle even for residents in their twenties, and I was three decades older, keeping the same pace.

While in Bakersfield, I shadowed a licensed family medicine resident, who would visit homeless sites, providing healthcare to those in need. I was still in training and not fully licensed. As much as I would have liked to, I didn't have any privileges to practice outside of the scope of my training program. Usually, one year of internship at minimum is required to be eligible for licensure.

I wasn't there yet, but every other Sunday morning, I'd deliver donuts to the homeless. In many ways, giving back (however big or small) enhances your drive to achieve more, to be able to deliver more, quite an unusual non-vicious cycle.

To wind down after my visit with the homeless, I would head up to Lake Isabella, located just outside of town. There I would spend time meditating and reflecting on the serene shores of this lake hidden away from the noisy city. The lake was lonely, like me, but it was peaceful in the way I also had become. It reminded me of the great French romantic poet de Lamartine's masterpiece called *The Lake (Le Lac)*.

While de Lamartine's ode to the lake in France captures his concept of love, time, and space, I would sit near the calming water's edge, and thank God that I was no longer homeless. I felt gratitude to have traversed this long, bumpy journey. I had dreamt of embarking on a career as a doctor, and I was doing it for a second time in a new country.

I was hungry, not for food but for my medical license, and a few months later, that dream came true when I successfully completed the requirements for licensure. I remember that day clearly. My nineteen-year-old son, Raffi, brought home the mail, and before reaching our front door, he did something he had never done before. He opened my mail! It was as if he'd had a premonition. He confidently pulled out the letter from the envelope and handed it to me with a smile adding, "Here is your long-awaited medical license!"

That evening, our family gathered in joy, and my wife asked Raffi to say the first few words of congratulations.

"Dad, after seeing you become a doctor for the second time in your life at age fifty-five, you made it difficult for me to give up. Now, I have no excuses to pursue my life goals and dreams. I should be able to be a pediatrician at least once!"

We all exchanged hugs and kisses and lots of kisses, typical of an Armenian family. And in that moment, all our difficulties and challenges along the road seemed to have disappeared. And as he promised, Raffi did end up becoming a pediatrician before sub-specializing in allergy and immunology.

My struggles to receive a California medical license reminded me of the seven years of famine in the Bible. However, after I received my license, I started a journey of seven (and several more years) of comfort and happiness.

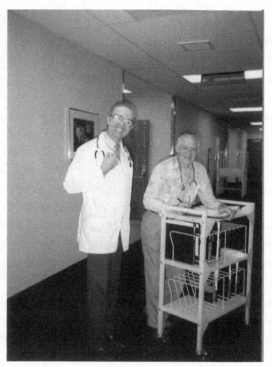

With Kern Medical Center's chief of pediatrics, Dr. Jess Diamond

Maro and Marly

In celebration of gaining my medical license, I stopped by at Zankou Chicken restaurant in Hollywood to buy some food for home, where Madeleine was making a special cake for me.

Margarit Iskenderian, the owner's wife at Zankou Chicken, was my childhood neighbor back in Tiro Camp. Every time I'd drop by their restaurant, she greeted me with a big smile and special food that wasn't on the menu. This time it was sarma (rice wrapped in grape leaves) made by her and her sister. I was chatting amicably with another customer as I stood in line, waiting to pick up my order when someone recognized me.

"Dr. T, is that you!"

I looked over to find an older woman staring at me, her eyes wide with wonder.

"Excuse me, do I know you?"

I thought of all the places I could have seen this woman, but I came up blank. To my surprise, she abruptly took me by the arm and led me to the back of a restaurant where a young woman was sitting with her child on her lap. Both looked up at me inquisitively. I still didn't recognize any of them.

"Do you not recognize my lovely daughter?" I shook my head, apologetically. She then said the girl's name, Marly.

"Of course!" I laughed in utter delight.

The older woman turned to Marly and said, "This is Dr. T, the one we've told you about who sewed your face so beautifully when you were a child!"

Marly looked into my eyes and said softly, "Thank you!" with her smile beaming from ear to ear.

Marly's case came to me in a flashback. I was working at the Aboujaoude Hospital. It was 1963, on a particularly quiet evening. But the calm was suddenly disrupted by the loud screech of a car. It stopped in front of the ER, the door opened, and we could hear cries of pain. A frantic father rushed into the emergency room holding his daughter in his arms. He placed her on a gurney, and I tried to comfort the child while washing the blood gushing off her face. The father whispered in my ear that Marly was playing outside with a Cola bottle in her hand. Then, in a freak accident, he heard the shattering of the bottle as Marly tripped onto the broken shards, some of which tore into her face and caused huge cuts.

I wiped her face with a sterile gauze and approached the deepest cut. It was a rather large skin flap starting from her forehead and running all the way down to her chin. I applied pressure to the wound and quickly explained to her parents that I could stitch her face, but that I wasn't a plastic surgeon. Pediatricians often give parents the option of calling a plastic surgeon for facial injuries of this nature. It improves the patient's outcomes and ensures that the skin is properly aligned, minimizing the presence of scars after the wound is done healing. We didn't have a plastic surgeon available that night. Marly's facial wounds couldn't wait until the following morning. Her father asked me to proceed with the surgery. He reassured me that he had full trust in placing his child under my care.

I started the procedure and prioritized saving her facial features. As I administered sedation to Marly, she gradually stopped crying and screaming in pain as we gently reclined her on the gurney to disinfect her face and get to work. I used the smallest needle and suture thread that I could find to stitch her face. In doing so, I recalled the image of another young girl from my childhood days, Little Maro. Maro was a seven-year-old child from my neighbor, who had sustained severe injuries to her face after an accident. I did not want Marly to suffer the same fate as Maro.

Maro was referred to as "the prettiest doll" by everyone in Tiro Camp, until one sad day when she was involved in a horrible car accident. In those days, seat belts were hardly used, and that's if they were available in the cars. She was ejected headfirst from the windshield and sustained severe injuries to her face. Several weeks after she recovered, I saw Maro walking around and was stunned to see what had become of her angelic face. Here was a young child with bright eyes and a beautiful smile that had been completely disfigured in the aftermath of the accident. Her wounds left behind uneven scars that changed her facial features forever. I often wondered if I could have sutured her wounds to restore Maro's beauty and smile that everyone admired.

As I continued to stitch up Marly's face, my goal was to prevent the detrimental outcome that Maro had to endure in her daily life. After sending her home, I asked Marly's parents to bring her back in ten days, to remove the stitches. Those ten days for me were anxiety-filled. I hoped and prayed that my procedure would leave no untoward effects. Even though I had repaired Marly's wound, my worry was tenfold, and my career could have been jeopardized then and there.

Ten days later, Marly showed up at the hospital with her parents. After removing her stitches, all that was left was a very thin, barely noticeable white scar on the side of her face. I was extremely proud of the way it had healed. Her father, who was a tailor and stitching expert in his own right, complimented my work saying, "I couldn't have done a nicer job, Doctor!" That affirmation spoke volumes for me.

Now, here was Marly standing before me, twenty-six years later and on the other side of the globe. I was dumbfounded and at the same time pleased to see what a beautiful lady she turned out to be. As for the scar on her face, well, it was barely visible.

Our families became close friends and regulars at Zankou Chicken.

Serving the Least among Us

License now in hand, I went on the interview trail. I received two offers for work: one at the Los Angeles Community Health Foundation (CHF) as a pediatrician and medical director and the other at Bakersfield Kern Medical Center as a pediatrician in an academic center. Since I wanted to stay close to my family at the now tender age of fifty-six, I chose to go with CHF.

Founded in 1971, CHF was located in East Los Angeles. It eventually became the second largest, most comprehensive charitable nonprofit clinic that provided health services in the USA. It served the predominantly Latino residents in Boyle Heights, City Terrace, East Los Angeles, Lincoln Heights, Bell, Bell Gardens, Cudahy, Huntington Park, and the Maywood communities. These were underserved areas of Los Angeles County and were federally designated as *health manpower shortage areas.*

When I joined CHF in 1989, the clinic was serving roughly 90,000 patients per year regardless of their financial status. In just seven years, we grew this number to 195,000 patients seen yearly.

Although CHF wasn't an academic center, it was a powerhouse, providing essential care to people in the community. Our homeless program was the second largest in the country and the largest in the state of California. Our mobile outreach team consisted of a driver, social worker, nurse, physician assistant, and a doctor servicing fourteen different sites and shelters.

In Tiro Camp, we had nothing but iodine, sulfa powder, and some gauze pads to work with. But at CHF, it was quite a different predicament; we had a multidisciplinary institution, and we were geared to treat almost any ailment out there.

The types of medical cases we treated ran the gamut. Some of the more severe problems included various types of trauma, diabetic and hypertensive crises, pregnancy with no prenatal care, sexually transmitted infections including HIV/AIDS, victims of child and sexual abuse, tuberculosis, and other communicable diseases.

Eventually, I would become the center's medical director. I was responsible for formulating, developing, and executing healthcare plans and programs. I directed and supervised daily medical operations. As chief health officer for the center, I was also placed in charge of development and maintenance of contractual requirements for medical services. I instructed medical students, interns, externs, and physicians in their training and worked to optimize the impact of our programs.

I went further by setting the clinical standards of professional performance for our physicians and medical support staff. We responded to grievances related to patient care that we provided, and I was one of the few medical directors to actually provide direct patient care in our center, as well as on the streets.

Part of my work included deepening our involvement in the community, giving lectures on health promotion and disease prevention at various academic and civic venues, which are two important aspects of a homeless physician's calling in my opinion.

I often thought about what the US homelessness situation would look like if the approach were similar to the core values used every day at CHF.

I dedicated half of my time to helping patients in clinics and homeless sites. The other half was spent as an executive, collaborating with the administration, the board of trustees, and community leaders. I was thinking that by further empowering the clinic, we should be better able to help the poor.

During this time, I worked around the clock, seven days a week, taking calls from hospitals, insurance companies, and fellow medical professionals, as I oversaw the well-being of all our patients.

I believe that many students and trainees who obtain their medical licenses feel an obligation to serve vulnerable populations: migrant workers, public housing residents, and the homeless on the streets. If I was able to inspire just a fraction of them during the course of my teachings, my calling would be fulfilled. And I feel lucky that this was the case in the majority of the youth I mentored. I had countless opportunities to help at-risk communities, and I've been proud to see the newer generation working with the same spirit to alleviate pain and suffering.

Before we can raise up others, we must rise up and empower ourselves. During my career, I empowered many underprivileged students, helping them with their medical practices so they, too, could carry the mantle forward.

The experience at CHF gave each of these trainees the opportunity to treat and help countless patients, many of whom were unhoused. Students become better doctors when they see, feel, live, and experience the effects of homelessness outright and in the streets rather than just reading or watching videos on outreach efforts. I knew this would carry much more significance and for a longer period in their lives.

They experienced firsthand the struggles of those without a secure roof over their heads, people with no financial stability, no control over their destiny, and many with no certainty about tomorrow. Some of the days we spent with our unhoused patients were too hot to be outside; other days we experienced the pouring rain, with no overhead shelter. Whatever the scope of the experience may be, all my students told me it was life-changing to be part of this exercise in awareness and engagement.

One of the most fundamental questions we must ask ourselves is the following: Is healthcare a right or a privilege? Shouldn't healthcare be available and accessible for everyone? The best way to empower any society at large is by providing them with healthcare and educational services. This is my calling in life.

With Community Health Foundation CEO Rudy Diaz

Dr. Juventino Villanueva on my right and Dimitri De La Cruz on my left

With the Community Health Foundation staff including
Dr. Lucas Casul, Dr. Renato Muncal, Dr. Luz Medina,
and nursing director Frank De La Parra

Some University of Southern California
students in our externship program

The mobile van team

My Last Night under the Bridge

Before heading back to the bridge for my last night in a tent on the street, I stopped in to see Benny. He poured us both tea into two chipped mugs and offered me a cookie. He gave one of the cookies to Scooby, his dog, who waited expectantly at his feet.

"So, doc? What do ya know that you didn't know before?"

It was a good question. What did I find out? I learned more about the physical and emotional problems that are particular to homelessness on the streets of Los Angeles. I learned that a day is long and a walk to McDonald's with a broken cart seems like it takes forever. I learned that a smile or a friendly nod makes a huge impact. But what I learned mostly is what I already knew—survival takes guts. Whether it's my grandmother carrying a crying child to safety amid a horrific genocide or Will walking five miles to the VA for his diabetes medicine or Benny living with a hopeful load of books to keep his mind sharp and his dignity intact—it all comes down to survival.

How could I put all that I thought about over these past three days in a few short sentences, so I only smiled and said, "I learned that an egg McMuffin tastes pretty darn good."

Benny got it. He patted me on the back. "You're a good guy, doc." I was incredibly touched by those simple words. Not to be too maudlin, he swiftly changed the topic.

"I think me and Scooby are gonna head east again."

"Really?" I said, somewhat surprised.

"Yeah, I got a girl back there who's been askin'." He paused.

"Maybe, I don't know."

The model example of the homeless person transitioning toward success was Benny. Every time I saw him, I would remember the following lines of a song by Komitas, a revered Armenian priest, musician, and composer, who is credited with a song called, "Homeless." A couple of lines from the song especially speak to me:

The heart of the homeless is troubled and wandering
Do not be harsh to their souls already so exhausted.

Back in my tent, I took out my notepad and started writing by the light of my tiny flashlight. By immersing myself into the unsheltered life, I got to see, smell, hear, feel, taste, and reflect on life on the streets. Sometimes, all it takes is to walk the same path as the ones with whom we are trying to heal. In fact, one of my dreams is to have a homeless experience for health professions students in their first year of training. I truly believe this would change the paradigm and result in advanced solutions toward the homeless state.

I am living proof that no matter where we come from, no matter how our path meanders through life, no matter who says we can or cannot, and no matter what our talents and shortcomings may be, we can still make a difference while establishing meaning to our actions. After being able to live in a proper house back in Lebanon and the success with my personal and professional life, I chose to go back to homelessness. I slept on the streets to remember what it was like as a child for me. I also slept on the streets to gain the perspective of the people experiencing homelessness today. Some nights were loud and frightening, but it was often the deathly silent nights that resonated with isolation and detachment from society, muted like post-traumatized inhabitants of Tiro Camp. Here these mostly lonely and silent human beings are misunderstood and misrepresented, terrified as if they've encountered scarecrows and wandering ghosts.

Leaving the Streets and Returning to Dr. T

I was packing up my tent and belongings when I saw the mobile van approaching. And there was Benny, having just put out the cones to secure the parking spot for the van. I saw my neighbors creep out of their tents and box homes with a certain amount of anticipation.

"Our boys are here!" shouted Will.

There was an excitement in the air that I had never recognized when I was the doctor in the van. Now, I could clearly see what our team really meant to Will, Benny, and all the others waiting in line. More than their eagerness for a health checkup, they were hungry to have human contact—I suddenly understood the depth of what we were giving beyond medicine—we were caring *for them* and also *about them*. These routine visits were more profound than I had understood.

A Machine Called Man

Although social media and electronic transactions help expedite our daily interactions, virtual conferences lack the depth of live inter-actions and the personal touch. What most people do not realize is when we miss out on direct interactions, we use less of the positive "community-building" and socializing neurotransmitters needed for proper human function.

For example, oxytocin is a hormone released by the pituitary gland responsible for regulating our trust, empathy, positive memo-ries, and communication. It is responsible for "gaze and visual focus" in an era when more and more people avoid eye contact. Meetings of the mind, soul, and body are therefore important for our collective health. In many aspects, moving toward electronic interactions may not be completely healthy for our well-being. Time will tell.

There are always friendships to be cultivated, information to be learned, and innovative projects to be carved out when meeting new people. There is also the excitement of being introduced to legends in the medical field. One of the legends I met during a conference was the inventor of the magnetic resonance imaging (MRI) machine. On behalf of the Armenian American Medical Society, we honored Dr. Raymond Damadian, a pioneer in radiology, with a lifetime achieve-ment award for his contributions to medicine. His prolific work was based on the concept that tumorous versus normal tissue have dif-ferent hydrogen-based signals that can be detected without the use of radiation. This has since become one of the most revolutionary tools to examine soft tissue like knee and shoulder ligaments as well as to diagnose various ailments including cancers. His full-body MRI scanner prototype now resides at the Smithsonian Institute, and the world owes a lot to his discovery.

When we met a second time at yet another live conference, I was pleasantly surprised to find out that his family was also of Armenian descent and originating from Kayseri. I like to believe that our ancestors' spirits are proud that their surviving children and grandchildren are trying to make the world a better place from the one they witnessed and left behind unwillingly.

Madeleine, Dr. Raymond Damadian, and me

The Fifteenth Anniversary of Armenia's Independence

Armenia celebrated its fifteenth independence anniversary in 2006. France called it the "Year of Armenia" and joined in on the celebrations. The French-Armenian Scientific Congress took place at the Academy of Medicine in Paris. Renowned University of California San Diego psychiatrist Dr. Hagop Akiskal and I represented the Armenian Medical World Association. Our three-day assembly garnered international acclaim due to the caliber and quality of the participants and attendees. The objective for this conference was to bring multidisciplinary leaders together to discuss and present on topics to promote peace and wellness in the world.

I was awarded Europe's special ribbon for selfless contributions in helping the underprivileged. My lecture examined the role of medical associations, their usefulness to their community, and the collaborative potential that transcends individualism. After my presentation, I was asked to moderate the remainder of the program, seated at a regally carved wooden seat. When the session ended, I left the podium to thank Professor Denis Pelerin, president of the academy. He asked me if I knew the history behind the chair on which I presided minutes before. I had no idea. He added, with a smile on his face, "Louis Pasteur!"

To which I responded, "Well, then, from now on, I feel myself pasteurized," as his smile extended to a loud chuckle.

Dr. Hagop Krkeasharian (France), Dr. Tadashi Goino (Japan), and myself sitting in Louis Pasteur's seat as moderator

Attendees of the congress: Dr. M. Timinski (European Union), me, Dr. Hagop Krkeasharian, (France), and Dr. Rafael Melik-Ohanchanian (Armenia)

My Stalwart Angel

In 2016, after five years of a heroic fight against breast cancer, I lost Madeleine.

I would like to describe the person who, more than anyone else, encouraged me in treating the underserved. That person to whom I owe so much is my stalwart angel, Madeleine. Besides her heart of kindness, she was an amazing wife and a dedicated mother of our two children.

Unlike mine, Madeleine's childhood and adolescent years were not harsh. The only child of honest, workaholic parents, she enjoyed the best conditions in life. But she was never spoiled. She was always loveable—and loved—at home, at school, and in social circles. That's because she was gentle and compassionate toward nature and humanity, and especially toward the needy.

Her presence always made a positive impact deeply felt by those around her and more so during periods of crisis such as changing countries and enduring wars. She faced those adversities in the same manner as she approached and planned out celebrations such as birthdays, anniversaries, and Valentine's day. Through it all, she never lost her giving nature and her everlasting integrity.

Even during her fight against cancer, her words, actions, and financial contributions were aimed at helping the disenfranchised. In that regard, one of her wishes was to have donations made to the Bird's Nest orphanage in lieu of flowers at her funeral. It was an honor to carry out this wish of hers, as that was the place that continues to have an impact on helpless children. After her passing, many of her acquaintances drew inspiration from this gesture and did the same.

Madeleine's charitable spirit continues with our children.

Oh God, may her actions and legacy be contagious to those of us that remain on earth.

Being her senior by a few years, I expected to pass on before her. We had been together for over fifty years, and here is a small excerpt from words I wrote about her:

> Before I met you, my life was full of darkness. But you made my life brighter with your inner and outer rays of light. Your greatest gifts to me were Raffi and Mariette.
>
> Your innate honesty, grace, and kindness have spread throughout your surroundings, so simply and naturally.
>
> Your virtue is hard to quantify or replace in quality.
>
> You symbolize the human spirit and serve as my guardian angel protecting me.
>
> My beautiful Madeleine, your wholesome presence transformed the fifty years we spent together, which passed by in the blink of an eye, into an eternal celebration.
>
> A million thanks go out to you, my love...
>
> It is hard for me to fathom that someone like you can pass away, after having planted so many seeds around you, that have blossomed into inspiration and goodness. Much like others, I speak of you in amazement and immense gratitude, as I feel so fortunate and proud to have known someone like you; the epitome of the best virtues. We will forever honor your wishes of keeping this family that you started united, and before anything else, aligned with our Armenian values.
>
> Your contagious warmth, inspiring selflessness, unconditional love and abundant faith

characterizes a unique phenomenon that I call Madeleinian. Although you were born into a well-to-do family, you treated people with your full respect whether they were wealthy or poor. Of course, you showed more compassion to the latter. On one occasion during a whole year, I spent without pay at UCLA, we encountered the same homeless woman twice in one day, a cold Sunday. The first time this woman was in a shopping center parking lot, and 4 hours later we spotted her again on the patio of a coffee shop 10 miles away, begging for money. Both times you took $20 out from your purse, which was a lot of money back then, and gave it without hesitation. Knowing that we are struggling financially, and perhaps also realizing my facial expression of minor shock, you turned to me and said: "We cannot forget that God blessed us twice, with two healthy children, according to our wishes."

You were absolutely right! After all we are all beggars in this world, homeless or not.

And to you, my Madeleine, I now say: "Your soul lives on forever, and your body has reached its destination. Whenever I visit your grave and have to leave, I never say farewell. Is it wrong of me to do so? I don't think so. Because you can never say farewell to your guardian angel."

A Return Home

The absence of Madeleine by my side created a huge void. I often found myself overwhelmed by a half century of memories: our engagement, our wedding, the shop where I was sending her the beautiful, sweet-smelling flowers that were a reflection of her, our family gatherings, and her smile and laughter. I had a strong desire to go and revisit Lebanon where my life and Madeleine's had begun. I think this feeling of needing to "return home" may happen to many of us who suffer a great loss. Alas, the loss stays for good and makes it known that it is irreversible.

With these kinds of feelings, I kept thinking about Lebanon with its four seasons, attractive sounds, stimulating tastes, enchanting perfumes, and captivating landscape. And thus, in the summer of 2018, I had the perfect opportunity to reminisce and revisit the past. It was my eighty-fifth birthday, and my son, Raffi, was invited by the American University of Beirut Hospital to give a conference on asthma and immunology as a visiting professor from UCLA.

From the moment we landed, I felt like Alice in *Alice in Wonderland*. I had changed, and my environment had too.

I wanted to show Raffi my birthplace—where we struggled, where I was raised, and where we all grew up. We stopped at the city hall and walked a few steps to what used to be Tiro Camp. The place had undergone dramatic changes and was renamed Norashen (or "newly built"). I achieved my dream of becoming a doctor, and Tiro Camp had become a city—a victory! There were electricity, water, and access to resources that I could barely comprehend in my earlier years. The wooden huts that we used to live in were now replaced with modern buildings, and St. Gregory, where I was baptized, had been renamed St. Vartan. A few steps away from the church is the Vahan Tekeyan School, where I once served as a trustee and physician and later on became a benefactor. This same school produced alumni greats such as Sam Simonian, founder of the TUMO Center for Creative Technologies. What's more, the leaders of the Los Angeles Armenian Apostolic church, archbishops Moushegh Mardirosian, Hovnan Derderian, and Torkom Donoyan, also hail from the same area.

Norashen is now filled with shops, restaurants, offices, and other necessities that any thriving city should have. To see my home, Tiro Camp, transformed into a beautiful and thriving town, filled with clean and organized streets, working electricity, and amenities that we did not have while growing up, filled me with immense happiness. I was also overcome by the emotions I felt for the Tiro Camp of my childhood and youth.

We visited the Howard Karagheusian Foundation, founded in 1921. It has played an important role in providing shelter, education, and food to the surviving orphans of the Armenian genocide. The foundation also helped hundreds of needy children from Greece, Lebanon, Syria, and Armenia. They provided refugee children of all backgrounds with food, shelter, education, and healthcare during the desperate times of war. They helped establish clinics, hospitals, and new housing all across Beirut and Aleppo.

Mr. Serop Ohanian, the current director, explained his plans for the foundation and what they were hoping to accomplish. Since 2006, they have introduced a seven-week summer educational program serving over 280 students and staffing 25 counselors each year.

The fifteen-year Lebanese Civil War and the ongoing war in Syria have taken a massive toll on the Karagheusian Foundation. But they continue to provide humanitarian, philanthropic, and medical aid to humanity.

Raffi and I communicated our desire to help out in any way and left the great Karagheusian Foundation after expressing our gratitude for their inspirational work.

While there, Raffi and I visited the Villa Audi Mosaic Museum in Achrafieh to attend an exhibition called "Beirut City of

Coexistence." It was created by sisters Lena and Hilda Kelekian and sponsored by Saad Hariri, the prime minister of Lebanon. Lena and Hilda were our neighbors, and like family, we've known them since the 1970s. I remember the sisters would arm themselves with artistic paintbrushes at the peak of the Lebanese Civil War, in stark contrast to the outside world that would arm itself with guns.

To my delight, I also met Mr. Hussein El-Husseini, the former speaker of the Lebanese parliament. He was part of the opening ceremony at Lena and Hilda's exhibition. Although it was out of character for me, I approached Mr. El-Husseini out of the blue and introduced myself. I thanked him for signing the Taif Agreement along with Professor Antranig Manougian in 1989. That treaty provided peace to Lebanon after it was wrecked by fifteen years of civil war. He remarked that both he and Professor Manougian were children of survivors from the Ottoman massacres of Lebanese and Armenians, leaving behind a legacy that would finally restore peace in Lebanon.

Ironically, Lena and Hilda are also grandchildren of genocide survivors. These two dynamic sisters commemorated their own life stories through art, with their collaborative and peace-inspiring art exhibition becoming something that everyone around the world should be able to witness.

It was Easter break during our visit to Lebanon, and there were no kids in sight at St. Gregory School. I was used to seeing the place full of children, talking, singing, laughing, and smiling as they walked from classroom to classroom, feeling spiritually and intellectually enlightened. I remember those children because I used to be among them. Raffi took a photo of me in front of St. Gregory. I proudly stood as an eighty-five-year-old man. But as I returned to my roots, I realized that I'm *still* the same kid inside, now revisiting those challenging days.

The hundreds of children who were nurtured by this place have now spread around the world and are enlightening their communities, thanks to the efforts of the staff here. I once again found myself as one of the fortunate and lucky ones who made it, reaching my impossible dreams.

I planted my academic roots at this school and know that I have reaped what I've sown, in a good way. Every step I take to climb the staircase makes it seem to appear the school growing bigger and bigger, and I shrink smaller and smaller. In the end, as St. Gregory School and I embraced, we whispered to each other, *arakelutyune gadarvadz eh.* We did it!

Standing in front of my school, St Gregory, seventy years later

From the left, executive director Serop Ohanian, me,
Dr. Soghomon Boyajian, and Dr. Raffi Tachdjian

With former speaker of the Lebanese parliament, Hussein El-Husseini

Roaming Around the Old Neighborhood

I enjoyed touring the Armenian enclave of Bourj Hammoud with Raffi and saw many familiar faces along the way. We enjoyed a delicious sandwich at the famous Falafel Arax and caught up with my dear friend and renowned watchmaker, Haroutune Karabajakian.

We later ate at restaurant Apo, located at Norashen. At night, we dined at Ghazar restaurant in the heart of Bourj Hammoud. If you have watched Anthony Bourdain's "Lebanon" episode, you will see him indulging in many delicacies like the Armenian pizza (Lamajune) at these iconic bakeries and restaurants. In the end, it felt as if we spent the day living to eat, instead of eating to live.

However, we didn't spend the entire day stuffing ourselves. I spent hours in the company of my friends and enjoyed some quality time with them. A few steps from Karabajakian's store, I came to Nanette, a store owned by John Nersessian, my classmate from St. Gregory. With excitement and great joy, we spent our time reliving the memories of our youth and revisited the photo we took of our graduating class.

The G. Ayanian & Sons electro-industrial equipment store is located in front of my old clinic, in the Antoine Jabara Building at the Dora roundabout. Most Beirut residents are fully aware that many of the streets, houses, bridges, and religious establishments are lit up by equipment purchased from this store, whose owner happens to be my friend, Paul Ayanian.

As long as Bourj Hammoud has institutions like Karagheusian; people like Haroutune Karabajakian, John Nersesian, Paul Ayanian, and my classmate and philanthropist Sarkis Demirjian; restaurants like Ghazar and Apo; and a philanthropic heartbeat, it will have enough food, clothes, housing, medicine, craftsmanship, and laughter.

Before departing from Lebanon, I mused, *Is this trip a gift from God, or was it me coming full circle with my life? Was this the beginning of the end of my life?* I didn't know the answer. But I did know that I had inherited the pain and suffering of my orphaned parents, and mostly had a sad childhood and youth. I can see it in the grim, unsmiling photos of myself and my sister as small children. Life was not easy.

However, inspired by my hospitable city and all its residents around me, I balanced out the devastatingly bad with the encouraging good. I have such sincere gratitude to everyone who has helped me, whether it is from close or afar. By escaping my own helplessness and underprivileged state, I was able to empower the lives of others who were facing the same difficulties. My life is like a coin: on one side are the painful tribulations of a homeless youth and on the other my happy adulthood.

Bearing these thoughts in mind, I visited the cemetery to see the graves of not only my parents and relatives but also renowned names in our history. The cemetery visit was disorienting at first, but then, my spirits were rejuvenated as the sun shone down on me. I lifted my head up to see a clear blue sky and took a moment to absorb my surroundings, the presence of Spring, smiling down on everyone in Lebanon.

And yet there is always more to do. The number of unrooted people is on the rise in Bourj Hamoud, in all of Lebanon, and also in the rest of the world. *Where is mankind's brain, soul, and conscientiousness,* I ask. Humanity, where are you headed with your increasing homelessness?

Back Home in California

When I returned home to Los Angeles, with both satisfactory and unsatisfactory feelings, I resumed my work with the homeless.

It will always be a difficult topic, especially for healthcare workers, the police, and the social welfare system as a whole. The city still did not have a complete infrastructure to address the needs of over 66,000 homeless people. In my interviews with the homeless, they always wished that the police would be less aggressive toward them. When I interviewed personnel from the police about their views on the homeless, they would tell me that more healthcare support and educational awareness are needed. I was glad to see that homelessness was clearly getting redefined as the condition and not the identifier of certain citizens in society.

I can say a lot about homelessness as I experienced it. As a physician taking the Hippocratic Oath, I was reaffirming to myself my childhood promise that I will always help heal the homeless unconditionally. Homelessness will always remain a difficult topic in society. From my vantage point, there are two types of homelessness: collective and individual. Both categories can be attributed to several factors.

Collective homelessness arises due to either natural disasters such as floods, pandemics, and earthquakes or to man-made disasters, which are avoidable and include acts such as war, incarceration, persecution, displacement, and genocide. I am one of those who struggled with childhood homelessness due to the Armenian genocide that wiped out 1.5 million out of 1.9 million indigenous Armenians living and contributing peacefully among the Ottomans in Western Armenia, now present-day Eastern Turkey.

Individual homelessness is often the result of behavioral and physical illness, psychiatric causes, unemployment, substance abuse, and abject poverty.

Regardless of the circumstances, homelessness can be blamed on the community instead of the individual. If people stop helping out one another, we will never advance as a species, nor will we be able to control or even end the crisis.

Even if someone manages to escape homelessness, the memories from that difficult period in their life will never abandon them.

Throughout my life, I took inspiration from Mother Teresa, Albert Schweitzer, and Maria Jacobson, great role models who dedicated their lives to help those in need. By simply helping, we can reach our own highest potential and make that difference. During my life, I have always tried to protect the dignity of human beings who are underprivileged.

As one of the staunchest advocates of our program for the unhoused, I pushed the pharmaceutical industry to provide us with medications, pressured the philanthropists and banks to donate more, and met with federal and local authorities to expand their support and improve their policies.

This basic yet successful formula is one I brought to the attention of the Los Angeles County supervisors. I asked for resources to do the work from anyone who would listen.

I thrived treating patients, but in my role as medical director, I also knew that change would involve having to navigate bureaucracy.

That also meant working with police officers, who are often the first point of contact for homeless individuals, including those going through substance abuse and mental health problems. I decided to do what I could to bridge the communication barrier between the two communities. The most effective strategy was bringing both sides of the communities together, by organizing health fairs and social events.

With CHF, we created and implemented a strong educational component as part of the regular health assessment and treatment visits for the homeless sites we served. We trained first responders and other police personnel in acute management of the homeless health crisis. You would think that these events would have a low turnout, but our educational fairs were known for their fun activities, musical performances, and food. They easily drew crowds ranging from a few hundred people to well over 18,000 members in a single occasion. Our program dissolved the barrier between the two communities and merged them into one larger entity. The program tried to replace feelings of apprehension with familiarization and camaraderie.

For safety reasons, we worked mostly during the day. We moved all around town but made a point of returning to see patients as often as we could to check their progress.

We frequently tended two homeless sites, the Royal Palms and Bimini recovery homes financed by the Mary Lind Foundation. Both recovery homes tried to help their residents gain the skills necessary to become productive members of society.

We expanded our homeless program from one location to fourteen sites, which made it the second-largest program in the USA at the time. I hope that others will continue to rehabilitate and empower this community with whatever they can afford.

Danish missionary Maria Jacobson with Armenian orphans

NIMBY

Nuestro Hogar or "Our Home" was a beautiful landmark building that housed eighty to one hundred homeless teenagers at a time. They could stay there until they were rehabilitated. It was founded by Mother Teresa's Missionaries of Charity and played an important role in caring for the homeless and poor of Los Angeles.

My homeless medical outreach care team and I would visit *Nuestro Hogar* twice a week to treat those who needed help. Brother Joseph, a member of the Missionaries of Charity, was the supervisor and devoted his days to ensuring the health and well-being of the residents. In September 2000 however, Brother Joseph informed me that the neighbors living in the Alvarado Terrace District were petitioning the courts and government to relocate *Nuestro Hogar*, since they believed it was causing too much noise and commotion in the neighborhood. He asked me for my assistance with the matter to save this sanctuary for the homeless.

I was approached by a teenager named Julio, who said to me, "Dr. T, where will we go if they close this place? This is the only place for us, and we need it for our survival until we can stand on our feet? Otherwise, we'll be back on the streets, homeless and aimlessly wandering."

Why would a center built for the purpose of helping others face so much pushback?

"Not in My Backyard" or NIMBY-ism is a major deterrent to housing people in Los Angeles. Residents want solutions to the "homeless problem" as long as it doesn't involve building accommodations, facilities, or housing solutions based in their neighborhoods.

I resonated with these teenagers who found themselves with nothing on the streets. *Nuestro Hogar* was their life.

I also knew desperation and misery; some of it was passed down to me through generations in my family. My friend from medical school, Moise Shems, had similar experiences with his relatives relaying horrors that occurred to their family due to their Jewish heritage and religion. Moise and I came up with the term post-traumatic stress disorder (PTSD) by proxy as our self-diagnosis. This is an epigenetic phenomenon, meaning that it is transmitted as part of intergenerational trauma passed on by those who witnessed it firsthand. Funny enough, Moise and I were the only two from our medical school class who would pass out at the sight of blood. We both considered our vasovagal response—or simply passing out—as an empathetic response to the gore and bloodshed witnessed firsthand by our parents and grandparents. This vicarious traumatization is now accepted in medicine as a legitimate potential problem in every sector of society.

Now, as an established doctor for the homeless, I wanted to break the cycle of intergenerational trauma for these youngsters at *Nuestro Hogar*. I took stock of the situation and wrote a letter to the Chief Zoning Administrator, stressing the importance of this center and its programs arguing that they would prevent greater noise and commotion in this and other neighborhoods.

I also testified in court to save *Nuestro Hogar* so that it could continue to help homeless teenagers like Victor Suriano, who came from Mexico. Like other immigrants, he wanted to live out the American dream, but he did not have a US citizenship or a valid visa.

So Victor snuck onto a train bound for the USA. The only spot on the train accessible to him was an open wagon with a large load of charcoal. After several hours of traveling, the train came to a violent stop and hurled Victor and the coal into the air.

When he got back up, he realized that he was now rolling on the layers of coal back toward the moving train. There was nothing he could do to stop from sliding underneath the wheels of this massive machine. Although Victor made a miraculous recovery, the accident left him without his left limbs and his self-esteem. It took years of physical, psychological, and spiritual work for Victor to regain some of his prowess back.

I sympathized with Victor because back in Tiro Camp, I encountered a similar accident on my way to school. I was at the train station, trying to catch a moving train. I ran to it and tried jumping onto the front door of the wagon, but when I placed my first step, I slipped and fell to the ground.

For a few milliseconds, which seemed like an eternity, I felt nailed to the ground and was petrified. I saw the train's wheels coming right for me and thought these would be my last moments in life. Fortunately, and by the grace of God, neither the train nor any oncoming cars hit me.

Terrified and shocked by my close encounter with death, I stood up. Still shaking from the fear of what just happened, I walked to the curb. I remember the metallic taste on my tongue due to the adrenaline rush that was surging through my entire body that day. Since that time, any train or even a picture of one stirs a discomfort and some fear within me.

I could have suffered the same fate as Victor, perhaps leaving most of my dreams unrealized. Life is fragile, and just as unpredictable, it's a phrase I have heard many times, and it is very true.

Those of us who have been blessed with favorable destinies must collectively try to help those who have had it hard in their journey. Victor's story is one of the main reasons why *Nuestro Hogar* kept its doors open as long as it did. I would often visit and examine Victor during my time at *Nuestro Hogar* and built a close friendship with him.

Victor's physical and mental health were beginning to improve. He went on to become a skilled computer programmer and, more importantly, returned to *Nuestro Hogar* to mentor and encourage youth in a similar situation.

Homeless outreach at Dome Village

Dome Village CEO Ted Hayes

Placita Olvera: homeless individuals waiting for
services by Our Lady of Los Angeles

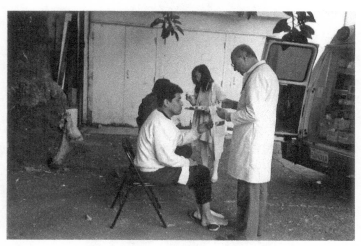

Providing follow-up care to a homeless patient

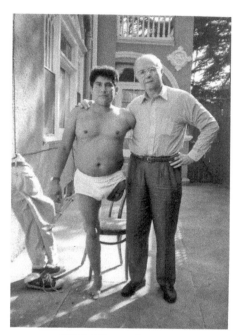

With Victor Suriano

Imagine

Imagine no possessions
I wonder if you can
No need for greed or hunger
A brotherhood of man

—John Lennon

I've spent time with the homeless in many parts of the world: the Middle East, Europe, Mexico, and the USA. I worked closely with the Doctors Without Borders (Médecins Sans Frontières) and believe that if we are united as healthcare professionals, we can impact the lives of the homeless more substantially. Anyone can make an impact by volunteering, advising, or helping in any capacity.

In 1997, our team traveled to Mexico, where we prepared healthcare professionals to prevent, diagnose, and treat HIV/AIDS. On that occasion, the Mexican social security institute honored us by recognizing our cross-border efforts.

In 2000, I visited institutions involved with homeless populations in Paris, France, and Genoa, Italy. There we exchanged protocols and strategies on improving the state of the unhoused. We spent nights on the streets with the homeless, in order to fully comprehend their needs and health.

The common denominator was that people were suffering and the private and public sector seldom found a way to cooperate. Treatment starts there.

Borders should dissolve for every healthcare professional when there is a need for healthcare. Diseases and misery travel more easily than humans across borders. We see it with pandemics, and I'm afraid we will continue seeing many more.

With the Genoa, Italy, Doctors Without Borders team:
Emmanuella Francini, Marika Viciati, me, and Dr. Bianca Costa

Stephanie Grant, Villan Duran, and me at the European Union

THURSDAY, JUNE 8, 2000 · EASTSIDE SUN · NORTHEAST SUN · MONTEREY AMERICAN SUN · BELL GARDENS SUN · CITY TERRACE COMET · COMMERCE COMET · MONTEBELLO COMET · MONTEREY PARK COMET · ELA BROOKLYN-BELVEDERE COMET · WYVERNWOOD CHRONICLE PAGE 7

Eastern Group Publications, Inc.

Health & Life Styles

CHF Physicians Tour European Homeless Services

By VARTAN TACHDJIAN, M.D. ARTHUR A. JONES, J.D. AND ROBIN WISEMAN, J.D.
Exclusive to
EASTERN GROUP PUBLICATIONS

A unique cooperative project was recently launched in Los Angeles that is already making itself felt in Europe.

One participant, Dr. Vartan Tachdjian, Medical Director of the Community Health Foundation in East Los Angeles, has been bringing medical care to the homeless for over ten years as part of the unique mission. During that decade, under the leadership of Executive Director Rudy Diaz, CHF grew from a single health center to becoming a bustling network of ten clinics citywide, winning several national awards along the way. Its mobile clinic now regularly visits 14 homeless shelters and other sites.

The other initiator is Ragnarök Associates, an international human rights law and policy organization in Los Angeles and Genoa, Italy. Its directors, Arthur A. Jones and his partner, Robin Wiseman, are both multilingual international human rights lawyers with over 30 years' experience in Europe. They are also active as mentors and advisors to European governments on human rights issues.

In Los Angeles, they have been instrumental in drafting and negotiating legislation and interagency cooperation projects. They are coauthors of the historic "Joint Agreement on Law Enforcement," entered into over the past eight months by police, prosecutors and the California Attorney General.

The three men met two years ago while providing services to the homeless shelter and became good friends. In late January this year, Arthur and Robin discussed with Vartan their project for joining together a number of their European associates and acquaintances in a comparative international law and practice study. The aim is to bring human rights organizations, homeless social services, medical and psychiatric outreach, law enforcement and government officials together to cooperate in whole new avenues of action to treat and reduce homelessness and its ravages internationally. All three agreed that by joining forces, they could make a difference.

The talks soon turned into action. Vartan decided to visit Europe. Robin and Arthur used their contacts to key organizations in Switzerland, Italy and France so for initiate a travel itinerary and a complete agenda with working documents.

In late February, Vartan was invited to the offices of the

Local Doctors Team up

Marika Vicchiatti, left, Solidarity Center of Genoa; Immanuella Franchini, Solidarity ...; Dr. Vartan Tachdjian; and Dr. Bianca Costa, director and founder of Solidarity.

with International Rights Organizations

prominent German politician Rüdiger Hess, mayor of the Frankfurt suburb Frankenberg, to help celebrate the mayor's 44th birthday.

On March 1, Vartan was in Geneva, Switzerland, for discussions with Robin and Arthur's acquaintances at the United Nations High Commission on Human Rights. He met with director of the Department of Housing and Economic Development Rights, Carlos Vilian Duran, and Division Chief Stefanie Grant.

He also met with the press officer for the Commission of Human Rights, Jose Diaz. The talks laid the groundwork for closer cooperation in attacking the problems of homelessness, disease, and mental illness on the streets— all in the context of human rights international law and its effective enforcement.

After that, Vartan visited two major homeless service providers in Genoa, Italy. Robin and Arthur have associates and friends in Genoa dating back some 25 years. One of them, Giancarlo Franchini, a prominent international businessman, has been concerned with the growing problems of homelessness and drug addiction, especially among immigrants and refugees in Italy's metropolitan areas. Franchini arranged appointments for Vartan with the Director of Social Services of the City of Genoa, Dr. Angelo Gualco.

They exchanged concepts and methods of rehabilitation and reintegration of homeless persons, efficient use of resources, preventive techniques and innovative approaches to delivering medical and psychiatric care. They also made a visit to one of Genoa's downtown homeless shelters, the "Asilo Notturno Massoero" (Massoero Night Shelter), and talked with the residents about their experiences and problems.

The second visit was to the internationally famous CSG, the Solidarity Center of Genoa, where Giancarlo Franchini had arranged for Vartan to meet with its president, Dr. Bianca Costa.

CSG has established residential rehab communities throughout Italy for homeless, recovering alcoholics, and drug addicts, and at-risk youth.

Vartan was invited to visit their headquarters in a rambling 350-year old villa, "Passolo," near the Port of Genoa. It forms the centerpiece of their local operation, with a full-service continuum including psychiatric therapy, job training, drug rehabilitation, community activities, and many other support systems.

News coverage of the Joint Homeless Services Project

134

Calling on Lawmakers

California Governor Gray Davis visited the CHF team on May 10, 1999. He brought the First Lady of California, Sharon Davis; speaker of the California Assembly; and later Los Angeles Mayor Antonio Villaraigosa. They were announcing the expansion of the "Healthy Families" program, which would secure health services for over 100,000 uninsured Californian children, and also commending us for providing compassionate and quality care to underserved communities. It occurred to me, there are folks who care out there, but I needed to influence them to act on those positive feelings.

Our CEO, Rudy Diaz, informed Governor Davis that CHF was the largest provider of health services to uninsured people in the USA. At the end of his visit, I thanked the governor for his services and wished for us all to have healthy families. I am proud to say that the expansion of this program has helped reduce mortality, morbidity, and homelessness rates. But programs like this can't succeed without robust and constant streams of funding.

I have always donated a portion of the moonlighting fees I was paid from working some extra shifts in other clinics. But I had to be smarter about getting funding for the needy. Then one day, my vision became clear. I needed to be a stronger advocate for attracting funding into this segment of society. Major donors would much rather have their name on a building (at a university) than the side of a tent/shelter housing a homeless person! I needed to learn how to tap into those grant-making efforts.

There is an art to fundraising. While charity is a beautiful act of selflessness, nowadays, *philanthropy* is the term that takes center stage. But many of the services offered through the latter term are based on self-fulfillment. Many benefactors ask to have their names on a building or a product, but nobody wants that legacy wasted on housing or assistance for the homeless. It is still fine to fulfill one's ego but to also follow through with love and the gift in question. I cannot count the times I have been offered a basket of strawberries from a field worker or a baked good from an inner-city, unhoused individual. Sometimes, it's the people who have nothing that give exponentially more. The obstacle for me is in helping the better-off individuals realize that the worse-off ones we help could easily have been us. To them I say, "When we have the means, we need to help those in need, even if they don't look or sound or like us."

I set out to find more funding sources. Financial institutions and pharmaceutical companies were making donations, and from that point forward, I was able to meet with some powerful dignitaries. My main goal in the short time with them was the elevator pitch, "I'd like to bring your attention to the underserved population. They deserve more than just money here and legislation there."

I met with two of the Secretaries of Health and Human Services, Dr. Louis Sullivan and Dr. Donna Shalala. Dr. Sullivan served under President George H. W. Bush and was pivotal in helping primary care specialties expand and serve the population. Dr. Shalala served under President Bill Clinton and even visited our homeless clinic in Los Angeles.

Knowing that her parents were Lebanese, upon meeting her, I spoke in Arabic: "Welcome dear guest, Dr. Shalala." She was a little astonished and asked where I was from, to which I proudly responded, "From Lebanon." She smiled and patted me on the shoulder, adding she understood that greeting.

During our conversation, she asked, "What is CHF's main achievement according to you as medical director?" I responded that we'd increased the number of homeless sites served, therefore scaling expansion of the number of homeless individuals treated comprehensively.

As she was leaving, I stated, "We can do more," and gave her a piece of paper with Mother Theresa's writing, which can be found at the end of this book.

At the tail end of 2001, our contributions to the unhoused population caught the eye of the Los Angeles County Sheriff. He invited me to discuss the homelessness crisis with his team.

At their East Los Angeles office, I discussed the overall situation with the sheriff and his team. Their main concern was to better understand the causes of homelessness, as well as find ways to curb violence and disobedience among the homeless. This was a broad request deserving more than a casual discussion, so I advised him to hold regular meetings like this one, because the solution wasn't quick or easy.

Before meeting for the second time, I asked Julio Morales, our mobile van driver, to bring the vehicle to the meeting with the sheriff. This would be used to demonstrate how our mobile clinic provided services to the homeless, and I recommended we mutually support each other's programs and expand the number of sites to reach as many homeless people as possible. I led the officers to the parking lot where Julio and I demonstrated how the van worked. This mobile clinical unit was ahead of its time because it brought medical care directly to homeless encampments. It comes with a medication chest, wound treatment gear, resuscitation equipment, and some amenities. When the presentation ended, the sheriff asked us if he could have a mobile van, like the one we have.

I replied, "When there is a will, there is a way."

"Can we perform minor surgeries in the van?" he asked.

I comically answered, "And when there are four wheels [which I pronounced as *wills* with my English accent], there is a mobile van!" The crowd erupted in laughter.

After the crowd erupted in laughter, the sheriff and his team told me and my team, "I guess this was the first time that we had this type of approach to treat the homeless."

He expressed his full buy-in toward the improvement of homelessness. At that moment, I realized that these various segments of society don't communicate nearly enough. Cross-training and collaboration between different parts of the community, such as government authorities and homeless sites, play a crucial role in reducing incarcerations, emergency department visits, and the spread of disease.

Our Medicine Chest

Our mobile van in front of Para Los Niños clinic

With California governor, Gray Davis

With US Department of Health and Human Services Secretary,
Dr. Louis Sullivan (appointed by President George H. W. Bush)

With US Department of Health and Human Services Secretary, Donna Shalala (appointed by President Bill Clinton), along with Community Health Foundation family practitioner, Dr. Don Garcia, and California congresswoman Lucille Roybal–Allard.

An honest conversation with First Lady Barbara Bush

Broadening the Outreach

After dedicating thirteen years of my life to CHF, both as a frontline physician and medical director, the mileage had taken its toll on me. I was nearly seventy years old, graying, and my vitality not as it used to be. I needed to make a change.

By 2002, Bob Lotvala, CHF's chief financial officer, became the chief accounting officer for the Community Health Centers of the Central Coast (CHC). I applied to work at this powerful clinic that helped the underserved populations in the San Luis Obispo and Santa Barbara counties and was hired as a doctor and director of the homeless program. Since then, I have continued to treat the needy in both counties of California with a team consisting of a nurse, social worker, physician assistant, and van operator. We see everyone from Salvation Army sites to those in public housing, agricultural workers, and those on the streets.

Ronald Castle founded CHC and continues to serve there as CEO for more than forty-five years. Under his leadership, we went to Washington, DC, in 2003 to attend a conference on homeless people, organized by the government. The fruitful exchange of information and cross-training exercises raised awareness on health provisions to new heights. After the conference ended and everyone returned home, we all had renewed vigor needed to push our program for the homeless to the next level.

During that trip, we visited the Holocaust Memorial Museum. On the third floor of the museum is a wall draped with the script from Hitler's Obersalzberg speech, which said, "Who, after all, speaks today of the annihilation of the Armenians?" On the floor below, there was another eye-catching display of various countries and the names of their citizens who played a part in rescuing the persecuted Jews during the Holocaust.

I noticed the name Felicia Tachdjian listed under Armenia. This absolutely stunned me since I have the same last name. I was in absolute awe of this heroine and wondered if the two of us were somehow related.

I still haven't gotten to the bottom of it and am trying to figure out if our families have any sort of relationship. However, I can say one thing for sure: for the well-to-do individuals, it is easy to remain silent when other people are suffering. And those who are suffering become more silent because of their own suffering. This learned helplessness creates a vicious circle that becomes difficult to interrupt. But we must uplift the global humanitarian spirit by helping out the destitute, the persecuted, and the homeless.

At Washington's Federalist meeting, to secure finances with the Community Health Centers team involved with the Homeless program. CEO Ron Castle (third from the left)

CHC

Community Health Centers
A Great Place to Find a Family Doctor

With thanks to our doctors...

You provide professional and dedicated care.
You treat each patient with compassion.
You make Community Health Centers proud.

Medical staff of the Community Health Centers

Home Less, More or Less

I returned home from DC feeling renewed, motivated, and inspired. That's when Dr. Paul Klosterman, a radio talk show host and member of San Luis Obispo's Medical Society, asked me to be a guest on his show. Speaking on behalf of the CHC, I was his guest for an interview during his live radio show.

He wanted to know what the most common diseases were among homeless people and where and how I treated them. I explained that most of the complaints were similar to the population at large, such as cough, fever, abdominal pain, and allergic reactions.

I also encountered many infectious diseases: viral, bacterial, fungal, and parasitic. We treated trauma, neurologic, and musculoskeletal cases. There were also a fair number of chronic diseases such as hypertension, arthritis, diabetes, and HIV/AIDS and a slew of mental illnesses due mostly to alcohol and drug addictions. Homeless people's exposure to terrible living conditions and lack of access to medical help make them way more susceptible to common diagnoses.

Along with my wonderful outreach team, we treat the homeless on the streets and in the shelters, churches, and special housing, as well as out in agricultural fields. Our van contains a well-organized chest of medications and a fridge that contains vaccines and insulin. For further help, we refer to the community center clinics, which are excellent primary care providers and resource points.

I should add that the most debilitating and common condition among the homeless is actually the state of homelessness itself.

Dr. Klosterman also asked, "Which of the two places treat homeless people better, your birthplace of Lebanon or the USA?"

I replied, "The homeless are homeless everywhere and therefore miserable regardless of their geographic location. Homeless people in the USA have better access to science and technology, but Lebanese homeless are better connected with their community and see more social interaction. From what I've seen, most of the homeless people in the USA live lonelier lives because they are often more isolated from society."

I went on to explain my methodology in treating the homeless. I explained to him my desire to see a more involved relationship between them and the rest of society. The best way for a person to heal is to reconnect with their community.

With a paralyzed homeless patient

Community Health Center's Healthcare Team for the Homeless:
me, Patty, Norma, Jennifer, Naomi, Frank and Leonore

*****

In my school years and professional career, I was always surrounded by the safety of four walls and my family. Now, in the luscious and green central coast of California, I spent most of my time in the open air, under natural lighting, and with great air quality and, of course, great food.

Most people think that life is short, but living your life to the fullest can add more years to your life span. I pass on nature's gift to the needy. This is why I find happiness when walking through open farms and fields and while driving through the streets.

We would check up weekly on our homeless and migrant worker patients in open-air sites across the cities of Santa Maria and San Luis Obispo. On many occasions, the patients would gift us freshly picked baskets of strawberries. I had enough baskets to share with my family, friends, and homeless patients back in Los Angeles. This was yet another example of why well-to-do people like me should help out the less fortunate ones.

When homelessness is portrayed in the media, it's often a negative image, dehumanizing those who are struggling to thrive or even to just stay alive.

As I continued my work, I felt frustrated when I saw homeless numbers on the rise worldwide. Our healthcare system needs continuous improvement. There weren't enough jobs to match homeless people who were able to work. For all the work that philanthropic institutions were putting in, along with NGOs, churches, and schools, it wasn't enough.

Goodbye, Benny

At the end of life, we will not be judged by how many diplomas we have received, how much money we have made, how many great things we have done. We will be judged by "I was hungry, and you gave me something to eat, I was naked and you clothed me. I was homeless, and you took me in."

—Mother Teresa

Born in a refugee camp from an early age, my main dream was to become a doctor to be able to alleviate pain and suffering affecting me and my neighbors. Since achieving that dream, I was able to heal myself and countless others along the way. I hope my life can serve as a source of inspiration to future generations of children dreaming to overcome their obstacles and getting out of their camp.

The last time I saw Benny was on Thanksgiving, when I invited him to our house for dinner. Madeleine had put together an incredible meal, including the traditional lentil soup. When I drove him back to Sixth Street, he insisted on making me a hot tea. Once again, I sat with him in his tent. Scooby was gone, but I saw his empty food bowl still in the same place. We started reminiscing about the past three decades.

Benny suddenly asked me, "What were your proudest moments, doc?"

I considered this question and then said, "I would have to say that my proudest moments in life are the successful careers of my son, Raffi, and daughter, Mariette."

148

Both my children are actively involved with community affairs, both culturally and in medicine. Raffi is a physician and professor of allergy and immunology at UCLA School of Medicine. Aside from being a world expert on rare diseases, he founded the nonprofit Children's Music Fund, which provides music therapy to children with chronic illness across the nation. Mariette became an accomplished artist with a master's degree in nursing management. After a long hospital-based career, she took a pause to help set up her brother's clinic in Santa Monica, which she has been managing for the past seven years. Her artistic skills and philanthropy have been gaining steady recognition in the art world. She also has sights set on furthering her art history education and publishing more in the near future.

Benny nodded. "They got a good role model in you."

I then asked him what his eventual plans were, and he replied, "Actually, Doc, I'm moving back to New York." He had once mentioned moving east, but that was years ago. "One of my old girlfriends reached out to me and visited me a few months ago. You have to meet her! She looks as pretty as Natalie Cole."

I smiled. "I would like that very much," I said.

"Yeah, she convinced me to move in with her." He shrugged.

I looked at his face; it was a mix of joy and apprehension. I asked, "You okay with that?"

"Doc, I gotta be. It's time I get off the streets. I been too comfortable here—that's not good for the mind."

I nodded. "And you have a mind that shouldn't be wasted." And I motioned to all the books crowding the tiny shack. He didn't look me in the eye when he said the next thing.

"Doc, I will never forget the compassion and care that you showed me and my friends."

I could see that his eyes had filled. "Benny, do you think I will forget you? We cannot and will not forget each other!" I was well aware that we would not see one another again—and the idea of writing or emailing was not likely. But then I smiled. "Since we are unforgetful, we must be unforgettable too." He chuckled, and as if on cue, together we sang Nat King Cole's "Unforgettable" song. We finished the lyrics both now with tears in our eyes.

After a few sighs and hugs, we both wiped our eyes and stood still for a while—in silence.

Raffi, me, and Mariette

*****

According to a recent United Nations report, 79.5 million people worldwide have been forcibly displaced through 2019 and 65 million children through 2021. This typifies the heavy burdens and the increasing numbers of homelessness.

None of us are immune: The strong today could become weak tomorrow, the healthy today could be sick tomorrow, the rich today could be poor tomorrow, the homeowner today could become homeless tomorrow, and the tides can easily turn another way.

We all have a responsibility and duty to instill drops or buckets of humanity into society. We can do this singularly, through a private or governmental organization or with a circle of friends by donating time, skills, and talents. In order to have a balance between the materialistic and spiritual sides of human life, integration of cultures is vital for those with homes and those without.

For ninety years of my life, I was in touch with homelessness. As a child in the refugee camp of Tiro, I was helpless and unable to treat those around me. Weeks and months would pass by in utter desperation for medical help, which never seemed available. I have been exposed to sick people from a very young age. Most medical students usually encounter illness in medical school where their main focus is not the patient but the illness itself. Treating illness has been a personal journey for me. Treating the disenfranchised person has been my mission. I continue to do that until now, thank God.

However, it truly takes a village to bring positive changes into this world. I was blessed with selfless collaborators, on the various teams I joined to fight for the homeless and against disease. As a result, I witnessed around me a reduction in homelessness, hospitalizations, school absenteeism, substance abuse, mental problems, and incarcerations, and there was a marked improvement in the number of people we made happy.

But who are the homeless? The men and women we pass on the streets, whom we turn away our gaze from. Some of them had ordinary pasts. Many others had extraordinary careers. Yet others were war heroes now forgotten, invisible, unproductive, and rejected by society. They are like myself, who grew up in a shack with no electricity or running water and barely enough food to eat. They are part of humanity.

*****

When I told Benny I was writing a book, he wanted to know what my message would be to the world.

I replied, "My wish is to see the world in a better state of health, with more humanism in humankind. And my message is:

By offering a piece of your bread to someone in starvation,
By offering a beat of your heart's pulse to those who are sick,
By dedicating years to your community as a form of donation,
And by pledging a sum of your money to the betterment of your nation,
Your time, wealth, and energy will never be depleted…
Instead, your generosity will perpetually be repeated."

END

Random Thoughts about My Remedy

According to my experience, healing others also helps heal ourselves. Concerning homelessness, there is unfortunately no universally standardized remedy to this global human disaster. The treatment is different from one country to another, one institution to another, and one individual to another.

Following President John F. Kennedy's words, I remind myself: "Don't ask what others can do for the underserved, rather ask what you can do for the needy."

Anyone is at risk of becoming sick or homeless at any given time. Like any disease or catastrophe, homelessness needs preventive and curative treatment. They say that everything starts in the home. This struck me as ironic. If everything starts in the home, what do we expect from those who are homeless? Hence it begs the question: *What* should be done?

As a physician specializing in street medicine, here is what I would do with my homeless healthcare team: As curative treatment, once I arrive on the homeless site, I examine the symptoms of homelessness in particular individuals as well as the group to which they belong. We then need to identify the etiology, which could be loss of job or income, accidents, untreated psychiatric disorders, diseases, addictions, or catastrophes like war, flooding, earthquakes, or, as was in my family's case, genocide. Then, we come up with the diagnostics and create a treatment plan that we execute mainly on the spot. When the appropriate treatment is beyond the scope of my ability, I refer the patient to the appropriate specialist.

Here are some suggestions from the approaches I used to navigate through this complex path. Throughout most of my life, while faced with health issues for my patients or myself, I was guided by health promotion and disease prevention. This phrase eventually became an acronym at the CDC and in federal healthcare vocabulary known as HPDP or hippie-dippie. It sounds catchy and encompasses curative as well as preventive components of healthcare. Communities and individuals have already been affected on a biological, social, and psychological level.

We are currently witnessing the most formidable example of lives disrupted through recurrent natural and man-made crises. COVID has taken the lives of more than one million individuals in the USA, and many more ended up on the streets; in some cities, the homeless population due to COVID rose by approximately 70 percent.

And then there are the intentionally passed around killers such as fentanyl. This synthetic opioid is fifty times more deadly than heroin, taking the lives of both affluent and impoverished populations at an astronomical rate and often resulting in homelessness. Nearly 2,000 homeless people died in Los Angeles from 2020 to 2021, a 56% increase from the previous year, according to a report released by the Los Angeles County Department of Public Health. Overdose was the leading cause of death, killing more than 700. We are failing in three major steps to recovery in the general population: detoxification, relapse prevention, and rehabilitation. Within the homeless population, the chances of successful recovery are even worse, as access to care and many other resources required to overcome these barriers remain unattainable.

But as history has taught us, even this wave of societal collapse will one day be a reference point in time. Some countries have fared better than others due to legislative and border-based strategies. Can we say the same about homelessness around the world? It continues to grow and defy even nations with programs to remedy this ailment.

Therefore, homelessness being a worldwide problem requires complex solutions on a global scale. The cooperation between governmental institutions (such as law enforcement, the educational system, and health and human services) plays a critical role, but much more is needed to achieve the desired outcome. The private sector also needs to contribute its resources from areas such as private educational institutions, charitable organizations, and non-governmental organizations such as community health centers. Ordinary individuals, family members of the homeless, and, just as important, homeless individuals need to be part of this contribution and solution.

When a student struggles in a large school or educational system, a simple solution is to place that youngster into a smaller pod. Replanting that mind and enriching it with tutoring, mentorship, more personalized teaching, and better oversight yield better results. Once that student acquires additional skills, feels empowered, and becomes more confident, the transition back to a larger school system or university tends to be more successful. Heck, we do this with animals we rescue before releasing them back into the wild. The homeless individual needs to regain the momentum, be empowered, and develop confidence to once again function at every level in greater society.

All the abovementioned curative measures are also valid as preventive treatment.

Preventive care is also extremely important to achieve continuous success in this population, young, adult, and elderly. I always pay special attention to detecting as early as possible potential homelessness in the youth. Teenagers are extremely vulnerable individuals. They are also at a tender age where self-image is immensely important to their self-confidence. Factors like peer pressure, hormonal changes, and volatility can easily distract them. Unlike younger children, teenagers make most of their decisions based on their formative years.

This is why I developed a pragmatic tool to assess and address ailments and risk factors before adulthood, in hopes of preventing homelessness. This tool is called *self-image*, and I presented it in Paris during the fifth Armenian Medical World Conference in 1992. We further developed it, and it was presented once again at the Grand Rounds of Harvard University's Massachusetts General Hospital in

2001. It can be used not only by medical professionals but also by teachers, coaches, family members, and friends before the adolescent reaches homelessness.

It helps measure their living conditions and health profile in a progressively engaging manner. We engage teens with simpler and less intrusive issues such as wearing seatbelts and helmets, leaving delicate topics such as sexuality and mental health for later after gaining their trust. The acronym stands for the following:

S: Safety
E: Eating
L: Learning
F: Family
I: Immune System
M: Maturity
A: Addiction
G: Genitals
E: Emotions

If any of the above categories raise concerns, these should be brought to the healthcare team's attention. This is what I used, but everyone else may have her or his unique approach.

I have always stressed the importance of unity and community within the medical–social circle. This has been the focus during my medical career, and especially within all the positions I held at cultural and social organizations, including the Red Cross and many of the medical societies to which I belong.

We need to start by acknowledging that these are people in our community, bringing people together, and socializing and fostering solidarity.

God gave us two hands, one for us and the other for the one who needs us. It can be done!

Now at the end of this book, the question is: What about ending homelessness? Can we expect to turn this around? I express my ongoing gratitude to official and unofficial helpers, whoever they may be. However, despite all that was done for the homeless, it appears that it's still a perpetuating and worsening situation. With the world population exploding from eight billion today to ten billion in a few years, homelessness is increasing despite all our efforts.

I've outlined here what we (outreach teams) realized during decades of work with our very limited resources. But the needs of this multifaceted catastrophe remain great. In short, I propose a three-part solution to this complicated issue. First, establish an international day of recognition for the homeless, such as Thanksgiving Day. Second, create a world rehousing organization similar to the World Health Organization (WHO), under the United Nations umbrella, which can be helpful in solving problems, locally and globally. Third, establish communities that have decent infrastructure, affordable family housing, nearby small businesses, dedicated health centers, branches of police departments, public schools, volunteer and mentorship programs, food banks, and sporting and cultural centers. By creating smaller, intact communities, some (maybe not all) homeless may fit in better. The homeless should be able to regain their health and wellness once they are propelled by nutrition, education, community connection, economic stability, access to technology, and housing, all in the same stroke. This is critical for the homeless individual to reach stability and independence.

Beyond the large ideas to solve this huge problem, we as individuals can make a difference by acknowledging those around us who are unhoused. A nod, a smile, or a hello can make a difference. As Will, my friend who lives in a box in a corner of a parking lot, once told me, "Dr. T., knowing that you think of me, even a little bit, well, that makes me feel good." And he looked away to not show me his welling eyes.

Benny and his dog, Scooby

About the Author

Photo by Cynthia Lum

Vartan Tachdjian was born in a refugee camp in Beirut, Lebanon, as the child of Armenian genocide refugees. His struggles were those of any disenfranchised, homeless individuals trying to gain traction in upward societal mobility. His dire circumstances and his surrounding community and its members pose many points of resistance toward the achievement of his dreams, to be able to heal himself and become a doctor in order to heal those around him. The difficult lessons he learns early on prove to become powerful examples of motivation, persistence, and success later in life.

Printed in the USA
CPSIA information can be obtained
at www.ICGtesting.com
LVHW041110230324
775320LV00006B/656